One Lit Step:

Devotions for your Journey

Lisa Buffaloe

*"Your ears will hear a word behind you,
'This is the way, walk in it,' whenever
you turn to the right or to the left." ~
Isaiah 30:21 (NASB)*

One Lit Step
John 15:11 Publications
Copyright 2016 Lisa Buffaloe (updated 07/07/23)

Visit the author's website at https://lisabuffaloe.com

ISBN-10 : 0692631410
ISBN-13: 978-0692631416
ASIN: B01MZ24R3S
Cover photo and cover design: Lisa Buffaloe
Printed in the United States of America

To my wonderful Heavenly Father.
Thank You for bringing me into Your family through
the mercy and grace of Your Son, Jesus Christ.

One Lit Step

The title came before I even started the manuscript. I could visualize the meaning of one lit step, could even see the cover design for the book, but I had no clue as to where to start.

On the day of my fifty-seventh birthday (gasp...) I pondered what life would have been like at birth if God had given me the outline for my life journey. If He had told me of all the hardships, trials, and suffering, I would have crawled right back into my mother's womb. However, if God had only shared all the good things, I would have jumped out with joy and excitement.

I would prefer a road map for life with the trail marked with all the good and exciting things highlighted. However, that's not how God works.

At times God shares His plans. God told old and childless Abraham he would become a great nation. God gave His prophets information to tell His people. The Bible blesses us with God's guidance, but for the most part our pathways are only lit for one step, and sometimes that step seems pretty dim and dark.

A friend relayed a story about a man attending meetings in an unfamiliar location. His room was a distance from the main location and the unmarked trail was dark. He had forgotten his flashlight, and fear overtook him when he couldn't see the way. He then felt the urge to run.

Running when he couldn't even see didn't make sense, but the prompting was strong. So, he ran.

As he sprinted forward, the most amazing thing happened -- lightning bugs in the bushes startled by the man's pounding feet took flight and lit up the trail.

In the same way, as we follow God in obedience, He lights our way. Jesus said, "I am the Light of the world; he who follows Me will not walk in the darkness but will have the Light of life" (John 8:12 NASB).

Take courage friends, with Jesus in our lives there will always be a lit step.

Along the way

With the weakening of my eyesight, I was desperate to be outside and enjoy the beauty of God's nature. I want to see all the Lord will allow me to see, so sweet hubby and I found a good rate on a hotel room and headed to the Ozark Mountains.

Arriving in the afternoon, we grabbed our water bottles, drove to a nearby trail, and checked the park map at the trailhead. We followed the markers to what we thought would take us on an easy jaunt to the lakeshore.

Although the afternoon was hot, a gentle breeze brought comfort and the dense forest provided shade. I tell ya, being in the hills breathes life back into my soul. I love the sound of the wind in the trees and the happy chirps of birds.

We happily tromped through the woods until we found ourselves at a caution sign warning the rest of the trail would be intense.

Uh oh.

We had taken a wrong turn somewhere, but feeling brave and adventurous we took the plunge and started down stone steps we hoped would lead to the shoreline.

Unfortunately, a little double vision is not a good thing when trying to traverse a steep trail made of stone. Fortunately, sweet hubby stayed in front and provided any help needed.

I consider myself brave, but I'll admit to being scared. Especially when we came upon an engraving by those who constructed the 338 steps – "Let those who tread here not forget, that these steps were not made of stone and mortar alone, but of sweat, blood, and agony." I am amazed those men were able to construct that trail without modern equipment.

Just walking those steps brought us sweat and agony during that hot afternoon. However, the beauty of the scenery and our time together made the journey worthwhile.

Life isn't always fun, and many times along our way the trails are steep, narrow, and stony. Obstacles must be overcome, and it's often hard to see where the path will lead, and we wonder if we can make that next step. Just as my sweet husband provided strength and stability during my walk, God gives comfort in His word that He will be with us through every moment of our journey.

Wherever your path may lead and whatever hardships you may find along your way, you can be assured God will never leave you or forsake you. Keep walking friends, the journey at the end will be worth the trip.

"Your word is a lamp to my feet and a light to my path." ~ Psalm 119:105 (NASB)

"You will make known to me the path of life; in Your presence is fullness of joy; in Your right hand there are pleasures forever." ~ Psalm 16:11 (NASB)

Stepping out in faith

I've created a few videos over the years for my websites, and most were very basic. When the few I made didn't seem to go very far, I backed away.

I really wanted to produce top-notch videos to inspire and encourage. Ideas and thoughts continued, but I didn't think I had the right equipment or enough knowledge or was very good on camera. Then I realized, I had been listening to the enemy more than I had been listening to God.

So, I made several videos and placed them on YouTube. Looking at them again, they aren't that good. They won't win any prizes or acclaim on video production. However, I was obedient to how I sensed the Lord leading. And if one person watches the videos and is led closer to the Lord, then it's all worthwhile. Even if one person watches and thinks they can do better, and they produce an amazing video that touches lives, that's even better.

A step of faith always leads to something worthwhile.

The enemy is the one who says we don't have enough, or we aren't enough, or we're just a regular person, but it's not about the not enoughs or the just enoughs, the reality is we are **more than enough** in Christ.

As Christians, we have God's power within us, and with Him nothing is impossible, and we can do **all** things through Christ who strengthens us.

Therefore, when Christ asks us to step out in faith, He will provide what we need, and following His leading is always worthwhile.

Take the step of faith to do what God has called you to do, because obedience, the step of faith ripples throughout eternity.

Whatever God has called you to do, step out in faith, for you are more than enough in Christ.

"The steps of a [good and righteous] man are directed and established by the Lord, and He delights in his way [and blesses his path]." ~ Psalm 37:23 (AMP)

"For we walk by faith, not by sight." ~ 2 Corinthians 5:7 (NKJV)

The Divine setup

I attended my first American Christian Fiction Writers Conference (ACFW) in 2006 and had an appointment with an editor. Unfortunately, about thirty minutes before my meeting, I received a call from my doctor. I was still in the battle with Lyme disease, and my white blood cell count was dangerously low.

I ran to the prayer room and asked for prayer. By the time we finished praying, I was late for my appointment. When I arrived, I didn't explain, I just tried to pitch my book. Needless to say, the editor wasn't impressed.

I was blessed to continue attending the conferences each year, and God blessed me abundantly by time with Him, with precious friends, time to learn, and time to spend with amazing editors.

In 2010, since I was spending all day on the airplane to travel to the ACFW conference in Indiana, I had purchased Jim Rubart's novel, *Rooms*. I started reading at the Boise airport and finished the book when my second plane touched down in Indianapolis. Jim's book is basically a metaphor for how God walks us through past experiences (rooms) on our way to God and His healing. God used Jim's book to prepare my heart.

The next day, I walked into my editor appointment. The same editor I had met back in 2006 stood, cocked her head, smiled and said,

"I remember you." Nothing negative, on the contrary very positive.

God had prepared the way. Then she asked two questions, one personal and one about my writing.

Even with all I have shared about my past, the personal question she asked wasn't one I had addressed publicly. I was surprised, but because of God's prompting through reading the book, I was able to answer without hesitation. The writing question also addressed moving in a different direction than I had planned. I knew both questions weren't just from her. God was gently nudging me forward regarding my past and my writing.

That night at a prayer session I kept my head down praying the whole time — I went from crying to laughing as I listened to the prayers, sang, and praised. I surrendered my ideas, my thoughts, and was ready to do whatever God desired. I was ready to face my past in a more open and vulnerable way than I had been before.

By the time I left the conference, three publishing houses requested proposals on my completed manuscripts. And my manuscript, *Nadia's Hope* was a runner-up in the Women's Fiction category of the ACFW Genesis contest. Since then, I've been honored and blessed to publish numerous books.

Through the journey and God's divine setups, I'm learning every step forward in obedience is a step closer to God's heart. Everything given to Him will be returned in abundance.

What God asks of us is always for our greater good, because everything we surrender to Him will be replaced with His loving, abiding presence.

Watch for God's divine setups; be open to how He is moving and how He is working in your life. Be open and surrendered and watch Him work in amazing ways!

What is God asking of you?

"Give, and you will receive. Your gift will return to you in full—pressed down, shaken together to make room for more, running over, and poured into your lap. The amount you give will determine the amount you get back" ~ Luke 6:38 (NLT)

What are you going to do?

Our world is held hostage by an enemy bent on destroying God's creations. Satan places lies in every wound he inflicts to make people question God's goodness. The devil steals, kills, and destroys then points to God and shrieks, "How could God do such a thing!"

Instead of blaming, complaining, and moaning, we need to point the blame on the devil who is to blame and then live as true victorious Christians.

We aren't going to win our battles if all we do is worry and whine. Let's stop sharing all the evil the enemy does and start sharing all the amazing things our God does.

We have an opportunity to make a difference in this world. We are each created uniquely, placed in a unique environment to make a difference for God's kingdom. As Christians, we are to be the hands and feet of Christ and minister to a lost and hurting world.

People need God's love, and they need God's truth. They need the bold, loving truth that will set them free for eternity. They need people who are willing to roll up shirt sleeves, put on the armor of God and stand firm for the gospel of Christ.

Christ's message is a message that saves.
Christ's message is The Good News.
Christ's message is forgiveness, mercy, and eternal hope.

Let's make a difference in the world by being the difference in this world – love with Christ's love, serve with Christ's love, and tell others of Christ's love.

"Do all things without grumbling or disputing; so that you will prove yourselves to be blameless and innocent, children of God above reproach in the midst of a crooked and perverse generation, among whom you appear as lights in the world." ~ Philippians 2:14-15 (NASB)

"How beautiful on the mountains are the feet of the messenger who brings good news, the good news of peace and salvation, the news that the God of Israel reigns!" ~ Isaiah 52:7 (NLT)

Let's love with Christ's love!

Snorts and snakes

During my teenage years, my parents lived on several acres where we had killed many poisonous snakes. I knew to be very careful when walking in the woods.

After my first year of college, I attended a large church in Houston. One summer afternoon, our college and career department had an outing on a rural farm not far from my family's home.

Most of the young women in our group were raised in the city and weren't quite sure what to think about the wild outdoors. The mischievous guys in our department told the females that snakes did not like pigs. Therefore, if they snorted like hogs while walking through the woods, they would be safe.

Upon our arrival, the trails were filled with the sounds of squealing young women snorting like pigs. No one got bit or harassed by those slithering critters, but I still wonder if it just wasn't because the snakes were laughing too hard.

As Christians, we have a real enemy. Satan is poisonous and out to steal, kill, and destroy. We have to do more than snort at the devil. We need to know God's word and His truth to combat against the enemy.

Don't believe the enemy lies you are defenseless, or you don't need to be prepared.

When journeying through the trails of life, don't just snort; use your sword of the Spirit to fight against slithering Satan.

"Therefore, take up the full armor of God, so that you will be able to resist in the evil day, and having done everything, to stand firm. Stand firm therefore, having girded your loins with truth, and having put on the breastplate of righteousness, and having shod your feet with the preparation of the gospel of peace; in addition to all, taking up the shield of faith with which you will be able to extinguish all the flaming arrows of the evil one. And take the helmet of salvation, and the sword of the Spirit, which is the word of God." ~ Ephesians 6:13-17 (NASB)

"For the word of God is living and active and sharper than any two-edged sword and piercing as far as the division of soul and spirit, of both joints and marrow, and able to judge the thoughts and intentions of the heart." ~ Hebrews 4:12 (NASB)

Feeling Unsettled?

Feeling unsettled? I can relate. After thirty-five moves I'm not sure if I get restless to move or am just paranoid another move is coming.

As I tried to rest and find peace in the Lord, Psalm 37:3 came to mind... "Trust [rely on and have confidence] in the Lord and do good; dwell in the land and feed [securely] on His faithfulness." ~ Psalm 37:3 AMP

Trust and dwell seemed to highlight as I pondered the scripture. Digging deeper, I found the definition of **Trust** (Strong's H982) is trust in, to have confidence, be confident, **to be bold, to be secure**, to cause to trust, make secure, to feel safe, be careless. The definition of **Dwell** (Strong's H7931) is **to settle down**, **abide**, dwell, tabernacle, reside, to make settle down, establish, to make or cause to dwell, to lay, place, set, establish, settle, fix, to cause to dwell or abide.

Peace came as I let these truths get into my little unsettled head. There is a boldness, secure, a feeling of safety in trusting God, and as I settle down, abide, and dwell with Him, I find the security in His faithfulness.

Deep breath.... Happy sigh....

Need settling? "Trust in the Lord and do good; dwell in the land and enjoy safe pasture." ~ Psalm 37:3 (NIV)

Joyful Blessings

How many of you have done word searches or looked for a character, animal, or for an object in a picture? Discovering what is hidden sometimes can be easy; others take time, and to be victorious in the quest, often takes effort.

I wonder how many times I don't see how God is working and the blessings He is leaving, because I don't look and search?

Every day God leaves joyful blessings for each of us. Every single day!

We have to watch for them, find them, make note of them, because they are there waiting to be found. Our days are filled with God treasures.

Please don't overlook God's gifts. They aren't accidents, or luck, or just something that happens. James tells us that every good thing given, and every perfect gift is from above, coming down from the Father of lights.

God's light shines on the darkness to show His beauty, love, grace, and joy. His constant gifts visually bless through the beauty of His creation. God's love and grace blesses through salvation through His Son, Jesus Christ. God's joy gifts through His Holy Spirit. Innumerable blessings are all around us. Let's notice, because EVERY good thing given, and EVERY perfect gift is from above.

Watch, make note, rejoice, and see how the Lord is leaving joyful blessings for you.

Heavenly Father, open my eyes to see Your good and perfect gifts. Help me to joyfully search for Your joyful blessings.

"Every good thing given, and every perfect gift is from above, coming down from the Father of lights, with whom there is no variation or shifting shadow."
~ James 1:17 (NASB)

In Christ

We live in difficult times, and everyone seems to be fighting battles. Battles are tough, and they sure do make us weary.

I have good news. We don't have to rely on our own power when we have the power of Christ living within us. We don't have to be strong enough, when we have the strength of the Creator of the universe living within us.

Therefore, let's remember the truth of who we are in Christ...

We are overcomers.

We are conquerors.

We are not condemned.

We are new creations.

We sit in the heavenly realms.

We are God's workmanship.

We have been created for a purpose.

We are marked with the seal of the Holy Spirit.

We are led in a triumphal procession.

We are heirs, and sons and daughters of God.

We have been given fullness in Christ, who is the head over every power and authority.

Neither death nor life, neither angels nor demons, neither the present nor the future, nor any powers, neither height nor depth, nor anything else in all creation, will be able to separate us from the love of God that is in Christ Jesus our Lord.

In Christ we have all we need for every need. So, let's rejoice in the Lord always. I will say it again: Rejoice and let's remember who we are in Christ!

(2 Corinthians 4:7, Philippians 4:13, 1 John 4:4, Romans 8:37-39, Romans 8:1, 2 Corinthians 5:17, Ephesians 2:5-6, Ephesians 2:10, Ephesians 1:13, 2 Corinthians 2:14, Romans 8:16-17, Colossians 2:9-10, Romans 8:38-40, 2 Peter 1:3, Philippians 4:4)

I've Got You

Feet dangling and scraping against the rocks, she clings to the side of the cliff.

He reaches out and locks onto her gaze. "Grab hold. Trust me."

But if she lets go, if he doesn't have a firm grip, have enough strength, or isn't trustworthy, all will be lost.

Again, he beckons. "Trust me."

Her choices are limited, yet she hesitates. Letting go is scary. She looks again in his eyes radiating warmth, love, and confidence.

Taking a deep breath, she lets go and grasps his hand.

He grabs hold and his grip is firm and unfailing. "I've got you. I won't ever let you fall." His words soothe her soul as he lifts her to safety.

Sometimes I get scared. Afraid of the unknown, I cling to the earthly and familiar. And yet, God beckons to let go, to trust Him and move beyond what I can see.

When God asks us to let go, it's because He has something better. He knows the future. Is God asking you to let go and trust?

Let Go. Trust Him. For His strong hands are strong and unfailing.

Heavenly Father, my feet are dangling, butterflies are fluttering in my belly, and what I can see is scary. Help me to remember, no matter what I see, and what may come, I am always safe in Your hands.

"With a mighty hand and outstretched arm; His love endures forever. So be strong and courageous! Do not be afraid and do not panic before them. For the Lord your God will personally go ahead of you. He will neither fail you nor abandon you." ~ Psalm 136:12 (NIV), Deuteronomy 31:6 (NLT)

Streaming

Sweet hubby and I checked the trail map and followed the markers to visit a river and waterfall. Excitement built as we navigated through the forest, fields, and rocky trails.

However, when we arrived, the river was dry, no water flowed, and the waterfall was only a rocky ledge. I was so disappointed. One of my favorite things is to sit by (or in) a river and play in the water clearing out any areas where the water does not freely flow. The visuals remind me of how Jesus cleansed us from our sins and gave us a new life.

We continued along the rocky stream bed and came upon a section with standing water. Even though the river was not flowing, the deep pool remained with life-giving nourishment. Once rain comes, the water will again flow.

There are times I feel so dry. If I were a stream, I'd be parched and empty. During those difficult days/weeks/months, I have to remember with Jesus in my heart, the Holy Spirit resides within me, and His living water is always present.

Jesus said, "He who believes in Me [who cleaves to and trusts in and relies on Me] as the Scripture has said, from his innermost being shall flow [continuously] springs and rivers of living water." ~ John 7:38 (AMPC)

Even when the way is rocky, even when our souls feel dehydrated, we can be assured of the life-giving, unending sustenance of our Savior.

"See, I am doing a new thing! Now it springs up; do you not perceive it? I am making a way in the wilderness and streams in the wasteland." ~ Isaiah 43:19 (NIV)

Please open

I so want to be open to the Lord to do His calling, to walk in His ways, and accomplish the purposes He has for me.

However, there are days I just want to crawl into a hole away from the problems of the world. Yet, if I close myself off from the world, I will close myself off to what God can do in and through me. Being open to God is the only way to have my heart open fully for His purposes.

Heavenly Father I pray...

Open Your children, Lord.

Open hearts that our hearts beat in tune with Your love.

Open ears that we may hear only Your truth.

Open eyes that we will see beyond flesh color, flesh beauty, and fleshly desires.

Opens hands that we may freely give.

Open mouths that we will boldly speak of You.

Open minds to be clearly guided by Your wisdom.

Heavenly Father, open me to be completely open to You! "O Lord, open my lips, that my mouth may declare Your praise." ~ Psalm 51:15 (NASB)

"Open my eyes, that I may see wondrous things from Your law." ~ Psalm 119:18 (NKJV)

"The Lord opens the eyes of the blind; the Lord raises up those who are bowed down; the Lord loves the righteous." ~ Psalm 146:8 (NASB)

Praising the Lord from A to Z

At night when I can't sleep, I'll often praise the Lord by going through the alphabet. I find joy as I recount the wonders of our wonderful God. My mind settles, my soul rests, and peace enfolds as I drift off to sleep.

Please join me as I pray and praise.

Praise the Lord God **A**lmighty, **A**mazing, **A**donai, the **A**ncient of days, and **A**wesome.

Praise the Lord who is **B**eautiful, the **B**uilder of everything, who is my **B**anner.

Praise the Lord who is **C**ompassionate, the **C**reator of heaven and earth, the God of all **C**omfort.

Praise the Lord for He is our **D**efender and **D**eliverer.

Praise the Lord for He is **E**ternal, **E**lohim, and **E**verlasting.

Praise the Lord God who is a **F**aithful, **F**orgiving, **F**ather.

Praise the Lord God who is **G**reat and **G**ood, and **G**racious.

Praise the Lord who is our **H**elper, **H**oly, **H**igh and lifted up, **H**ealer., the Lord of **H**osts.

Praise the Lord who is **I** Am.

Praise the Lord who is **J**ehovah, **J**oy and a **J**ust **J**udge.

Praise the Lord who is **K**ing and is **K**ind.

Praise the Lord, who is **L**oving **L**ord of all, **L**ord our God.

Praise the Lord who is **M**ighty, the **M**ost High, **M**aker, and **M**arvelous.

Praise the Lord who is **N**ame above all names, Jehovah **N**issi, the God over all **N**ations.

Praise the Lord who is **O**mnipotent, **O**mniscient, the **O**nly true God.

Praise the Lord who is **P**owerful, the **P**otter, my **P**eace.

Praise the Lord who **Q**uiets us with His love.

Praise the Lord who is **R**ighteous, my **R**ock, my **R**edeemer.

Praise the Lord who is **S**trong, **S**avior, **S**overeign Lord, **S**hield, and **S**alvation.

Praise the Lord who is **T**rue, **T**riumphant, and **T**imeless.

Praise the Lord who is **U**nfailing, **U**pright, with all **U**nderstanding.

Praise the Lord who is **V**ictorious.

Praise the Lord who is **W**onderful, **W**ise and **W**orthy of all **W**orship.

Praise the Lord who is e**X**alted and e**X**traordinary.

Praise the Lord who is **Y**ahweh.

Praise the Lord who is God of **Z**ion, **Z**ealous for his people.

Praise the Lord with me. Let all the earth praise the Lord! What descriptions of our wonderful God can you add to my alphabet list?

"I am the Alpha and the Omega, the Beginning and the End, says the Lord, who is and who was and who is to come, the Almighty." ~ Revelation 1:8 (NKJV)

Looking for God's provision

I wonder how often I miss how God works and provides because I'm so busy watching for the ways I think He will work and provide?

When God provides, He has used some interesting and unusual methods.

God's provision has come...

Through quail – Exodus 16:13.

Through manna – Exodus 16:14-36.

Through the mouth of a fish – Matthew 17:27.

Through loaves and fishes – Mark 6:41-44.

Through the enemy's camp – 2 Kings 7.

By the ravens – 1 Kings 17:6.

Through oil that doesn't end – 2 Kings 4:1-7.

Through spotted and speckled sheep – Genesis 30:25-43.

From water gushing from a rock – Exodus 1:1-7.

How many times has God provided and I failed to notice? How many times was I so busy watching the sky for quail or ravens that I missed the manna? How many times was I so busy fishing for that one fish that I missed the empty enemy camp behind me?

How many times have I prayed for God to work in one way, and missed the million ways He did work and continues to work?

Heavenly Father I don't want to miss how You provide. Open my eyes to see how You work and how You meet every need. Forgive me for staring so hard at how I think You'll move that I miss seeing Your footprints of provision all around me.

Call in Truth

"The Lord is near to all who call upon Him, to all who call upon Him in truth." ~ Psalm 145:18 (NASB)

The Lord is near to all who call upon Him. Such a blessed thought! The Lord is near. *Happy sigh*

However, the second part of the verse is often forgotten. God is near to those who call upon Him in truth. Truth is necessary to communicate with The One who is Truth.

Pretending doesn't work. When the heart is troubled, angry, or frustrated, cleaning up prayer to be more presentable doesn't work. God knows our hearts. He knows every thought and every emotion.

Be honest! He already knows. Do you realize what a blessing it is to be completely honest? God made you, loves you, and knows you, you can honestly come to Him with everything.

Be honest with your concerns or worries, with whatever you are feeling, because in that honesty God can reveal the lies of the enemy.

In truth, the Truth can be revealed. In truth, The Truth can speak the truth into your situation and your soul.

Call to God. Call in truth, and the Lord will be near. His tender words beckon, "Call to Me and I will answer you, and I will tell you great and mighty things, which you do not know" (Jeremiah 33:3, NASB). Call to God. He's waiting. His love is waiting for you!

Trail Markers

As of December 2016, I've moved thirty-five times. The trail has been a wild ride filled with ups and downs, good and bad, hardship and fun. Some memories make me smile, others make me shudder, and all make me grateful for a forgiving, restoring God.

During the Israelites journey to the Promised Land, God had them place stones to remember the rescues He had made and the great things He had done. I wonder what it would be like if we did the same?

What if we had spiritual markers, gratitude stones that marked our trails? Wouldn't that be amazing? As we watched (and made note) where God worked and is working, we would look back and see the firm foundation of the faithfulness of God. Our marker stones would build on the past for our present and future. Our steps would become more sure because we would be grounded in the sureness of God.

The Bible tells us every good thing given and every perfect gift comes from God (James 1:17). Every good thing. Every single one. The beauty your eyes see, the pleasing sounds your ears hear, the food you eat, the shelter you have, the sweet memories cherished in your heart, every blessing is a blessing from God. He pours out His love upon us all every single moment of every single day.

We make the choice to notice, to remember, and to thank God for the good along our journeys.

I want to do that! I want to leave trail markers that remind me of God's faithfulness and show others the protection and provision of our wonderful God.

Want to join me?

Heavenly Father, thank You for the amazing blessings You have given me along my journey. Please forgive me when I didn't notice or pay attention. Please remind me of Your past faithfulness and open my eyes to see and my ears to hear all the wonderful ways You are working now. Thank You, Father. Thank You for all You have done and all You will do and thank You most of all for being You!

"It is good to give thanks to the Lord, and to sing praises to Your name, O Most High; to declare Your lovingkindness in the morning, and Your faithfulness every night." ~ Psalm 92:1-2 (NKJV)

Doing your best

I love watching the Olympics. I'm so amazed at athletes who train and strive to be the best at their sport.

To advance to the finals, the athletes must compete in various heats and semi-finals. In the 2012 Olympics, Gold medalist Michael Phelps raced in an early event. All cameras were trained on him as he easily finished in first place. Michael didn't break records with his swim; he just wanted to make sure he advanced. He won his heat, but those who finished behind him didn't move on to the next round.

Did the other athletes think if they stayed close enough to Michael, they would move to the next level? Did they keep their eyes on Michael instead of striving to do their best?

Which causes me to wonder ... are we keeping our eyes on God or those around us? Are we comparing our best to what others do, or what God has called us to do?

Heavenly Father, help me to do my absolute best at what You have called me to accomplish. Help me not to compare myself to others, but keep focused solely on You.

"Do you not know that those who run in a race all run, but only one receives the prize? Run in such a way that you may win." ~ 1 Corinthians 9:24 (NASB)

I want that!

I'll admit there are some things I really wish would happen, some things I have waited and wanted for years. I'm patient at times, not so much on some days, because some days are hard and so very long and the wait is really long, really, really, *really long*... and did I mention it's been a **really** long time?

Sigh...

Something happened to an author friend of mine and I wanted what she got. I want that!

Seeing the success of those who succeed seems to make the wait of those waiting on their success even harder and longer. And yet there are so **many more** people who are waiting, hoping, and fighting through each and every day, who didn't get what they hoped they'd get, who wonder if they will ever get what they are hoping they will get, and are questioning why they should wait when the wait takes SO VERY LONG!

Sigh...

As I sat at my desk staring at the computer screen having a small pity party, contemplating my friend's success (which by the way is *very* deserved), I remembered what Jesus said in Luke 6:31 "Treat others the same way you want them to treat you" and Paul told us to "rejoice with those who rejoice."

Hmmm...

So, I pushed aside my sadness, congratulated my friend, and passed on her good news to others.

An interesting thing happened ... **as I shared in her joy, I felt a spark of joy**.

I realized, one of the fruits the Holy Spirit gifts us with is joy, and the joy of the Lord is our strength, and Jesus said, "give and it will be given to you."

That is what I really want – I want to share in the joy of Jesus. So, by gifting the joy of Jesus, I am gifted with the full throttle, pressed down, shaken together joy of Jesus. Therefore, while I continue to wait, I will rejoice with those who rejoice, and I will treat others the way I want to be treated by gifting them with the joy of Jesus.

Do you want that? Do you want the joy of Jesus? Get Jesus, you get joy. Gift the joy of Jesus, and your joy multiplies!

"Give and it will be given to you. They will pour into your lap a good measure—pressed down, shaken together, and running over [with no space left for more]. For with the standard of measurement you use [when you do good to others], it will be measured to you in return." ~ Luke 6:38 (AMP)

Who you know

Have you ever thought... if only *that* person would notice me (help me, care about me, provide for me, love me...), then I would be happy (successful, have the money needed, get the job I want, have my problems solved...).

It's so easy to think people will provide the answers to our problems; that someone, *anyone*, will come through with the money needed, or the connection we need to be properly connected.

Someone needs to know, someone needs to remember, and that someone is me.

Wherever you are, God knows.

Whatever circumstance you are in, God knows.

Whatever need you need, God knows.

It's not who you know, but WHO you know.

God - The One who love you, knows you best and always knows where you are, He has every resource for every provision and every need.

God knows where you are, He knows what you need, and HE has everything needed for you. For me, and hopefully for you, that is such good news that we can rest knowing we are known and forever loved!

Cease striving, know that I am God. I know what you need before you ask Me. I've set apart the faithful servant for Myself; I hear you when you call. I will supply all your needs. (Psalm 46:10, Matthew 6:8, Psalm 4:3, Philippians 4:19)

Giving Christ

God has given me grace, mercy, unfailing love, and blessed me in ways too numerous to count. A passion burns in me to do more for God's Kingdom, and I beg and plead and ask how can I give more to Him.

God's word reminds me to tell others how I and others can help, how we can all tell others about His love.

Through our actions or through giving to neighbors, our community, our church, and/or Christian ministries, we can share hope.

Your smile, your caring touch, one hug, one dollar, one act of kindness can make a difference in this world. You can make sure a child doesn't go hungry one more day. You can give wheelchairs to lift someone off the ground who can only crawl. You can help spread the Gospel of Christ across the nations. You can help those who are persecuted for their faith.

You can make a difference. If not financially, you can volunteer to help, and most importantly you can pray.

Please don't just turn away, don't ignore when God knocks on your heart. This isn't about guilting you into doing something; this is a call to bless so you can be blessed. In the beauty of giving in God's kingdom, we are always blessed by blessing.

A hungry world needs the Bread of Life. A thirsty world needs The Living Water. A world without peace needs the Prince of Peace.

Gift others with the gift of God's grace and mercy. Give Life. Give hope. Give caring. Give yourself. Give Christ.

"Give, and you will receive. Your gift will return to you in full pressed down, shaken together to make room for more, running over, and poured into your lap. The amount you give will determine the amount you get back." ~ Luke 6:38 (NLT)

"Then the King will say to those on his right, 'Come, you who are blessed by my Father, inherit the Kingdom prepared for you from the creation of the world. For I was hungry, and you fed me. I was thirsty, and you gave me a drink. I was a stranger, and you invited me into your home. I was naked, and you gave me clothing. I was sick, and you cared for me. I was in prison, and you visited me.'" ~ Matthew 25:34-36 (NLT)

Reverse

Ready for a test drive in a new shiny car, I sat behind the steering wheel while the salesman rattled off the automobile's features. After placing the keys in the ignition, I put the car in what I thought was reverse. A tap on the accelerator sent the car lurching forward and over a small concrete barrier. Although I was thoroughly humiliated, thankfully the car was fine.

Sometimes reverse is the proper mode of transportation. However, there have been times I've found myself moving backwards when I should have been moving forward.

In life's difficulties it seems easier to run and hide, because the world will say there are "some" things that will never allow recovery and there isn't any reason to hope. Fortunately, there is always a reason for hope and to move forward, because God is so much bigger than the world and SO MUCH BIGGER than a worldly viewpoint.

The world can't fix things, but God can.

There is nothing too hard for our God.

The One who made you can remake you.

The One who created you can recreate you.

The One who is life grants new life.

The One who loves you doesn't stop loving you.

The One who wants the best plans for you will provide a way for those plans to come to fruition.

Go forward with God who renews, redeems, and restores. Let God reverse the past to a new eternal, exciting, future with Him.

You are a new creation, raised up and seated in the heavenlies, blessed with every spiritual blessing, and made alive together with Christ, therefore move forward in the grace and power of God!

"Therefore, if anyone is in Christ, he is a new creature; the old things passed away; behold, new things have come." ~ 2 Corinthians 5:17 (NASB)

"Therefore, if you have been raised up with Christ, keep seeking the things above, where Christ is, seated at the right hand of God." ~ Colossians 3:1 (NASB)

"Blessed be the God and Father of our Lord Jesus Christ, who has blessed us with every spiritual blessing in the heavenly places in Christ, just as He chose us in Him before the foundation of the world, that we would be holy and blameless before Him. In love He predestined us to adoption as sons through Jesus Christ to Himself, according to the kind intention of His will." ~ Ephesians 1:3-5 (NASB)

We have been made "alive together with Christ (by grace you have been saved), and raised us up with Him, and seated us with Him in the heavenly places in Christ Jesus." ~ Ephesians 2:5-6 (NASB)

Too little, not enough

Do you ever wonder if you really have anything to offer God? It's easy to get lost in the mass of humanity, and far-too-easy to feel like we have so little to give that will make a difference or an impact in the world.

I have good news! With God's touch, ordinary becomes extraordinary. God takes the small and makes them great. Gideon, the least from the smallest tribe, became a mighty warrior. Little David became a giant slayer. Average fishermen became mighty fishers for God's kingdom.

When there doesn't seem to be enough, Jesus multiplies what is given to Him. Only five loaves and two small fish fed 5000 men (plus women and children). All ate and were satisfied, and the disciples picked up twelve basketfuls of broken pieces that were left over (Matthew 14:15-21).

Only seven loaves and a few small fish fed 4000 men (plus women and children). All ate and were satisfied and afterward the disciples picked up seven basketfuls of broken pieces that were left over. (Matthew 15:30-39)

Too little became more than enough. So little became so much. With Jesus, our little lives, our small offerings, becomes food for the hungry, giant-slaying, life giving, fully satisfying, God-praising miracles.

Give Jesus your life and your offerings and watch the amazing things He will do in you and through you!

"Give, and it will be given to you. They will pour into your lap a good measure—pressed down, shaken together, and running over. For by your standard of measure it will be measured to you in return. For nothing is impossible for God. He is able to do exceedingly abundantly above all that we ask or think, according to the power that works in us." ~ Luke 6:38 (NASB), Luke 1:37 (NASB), Ephesians 3:20 (NKJV)

Good, good Father

The world is a mess. People are hurting, angry, crazy, and downright messy. But please remember our God is doing AMAZING things. Every. Single. Day. our God is doing amazing things.

Prayers are being answered. Comfort is being given. Provision is being made. Lives are being changed and hope runs eternal.

Our God is a good, good Father. He cares, He loves, He reaches out and calls to the lost, His heart is tender toward all He has made. There is no problem and no situation too big for our God. There is nothing beyond His reach. God is just and righteous. Evil will be punished. And someday soon, tears will be wiped away and eternal safety given to His children.

Whatever you face, whatever your need, run to God, because He is a good, good Father. His arms are open wide to hold you and carry you through. Oh, He is a good, **good** Father.

"Like a shepherd, he will care for his flock, gathering the lambs in his arms, hugging them as he carries them, leading the nursing ewes to good pasture." ~ Isaiah 40:11 (MSG)

The Perfect Place

I adore hiking in the mountains. Over the years, I've been blessed to walk trails around the country. The clean outdoor air clears my lungs and my mind. I feel closer to the Lord in the stillness of God's nature.

The times I've had those opportunities are joy-filled... Best. Days. Ever!

Since I was a young girl, I've wanted to live in a cabin in the mountains with a small stream, creek or river nearby. Other friends tell me they would love a place by the ocean, others prefer the city life.

Regardless of the location, I think most of us can envision a perfect place, a place where we can find peace and belonging, a place that would restore our souls.

As I was praying and pondering this life-long longing, I felt the Lord impress on my spirit that it's not a place, but in His presence where joy is found. God is our peace, He is our joy, He is the only One who can restore souls. He is the living water, the home for our hearts, the perfect place where we abide in His unfailing, perfect love.

Looking for that perfect place? The perfect place is found in God's perfect presence.

"I'm asking God for one thing, only one thing: to live with him in his house my whole life long. I'll contemplate his beauty; I'll study **at his feet**. That's the only quiet, secure place in a noisy world, **the perfect getaway**, far from the buzz of traffic." ~ Psalm 27:4-5 (MSG) (Bold mine)

"My help and glory are in God—granite-strength and safe-harbor-God—so trust him absolutely, people; lay your lives on the line for him. **God is a safe place to be**." ~ Psalm 62:7-8 (MSG) (Bold mine)

God and Generals

I've been burdened, driven, and desperate to do more for God. One night back in June, I woke with the words, "God and generals" running through my mind. I had no clue what that meant but made a note to pray and see what God would reveal.

For over two months I couldn't find an answer, and then finally God brought clarity. I've been overly focused on the earthly battles – the devastating needs around the world.

God blessed with a visual. I saw myself on a battlefield, looking at the overwhelming needs. I'd let out a scream, and then run around trying to put out fires with a little pail of water. I would see another need and then another, and another, and another, and not accomplish much of anything other than screaming, running, and making little splashes.

Then God revealed He already has a fire team lined up to put out the fires and I'm merely getting in the way.

Instead of running around like a chicken with my head cut off, I need to be talking to God, my General, and follow His battle plan.

A General sees the overall picture, and he knows where everyone needs to be during every part of the battle. Each soldier has an assignment where they can be most effective.

Can you imagine the chaos if everyone did what he thought he should do? Yes, you would see Lisa running around screaming, trying to help, and merely getting in the way.

When Jesus walked the earth, He never ran, never seemed to be stressed-out by the needs and neediness of people – He kept focused on God and followed His commands.

As a Christian my job is to follow Jesus. God is my General. I'm not responsible for fixing the world's problems because I can't fix the world's problems whereas God can fix every problem. I can pray because my prayers are never limited. Where I go and what I do ... I must follow Him.

As His soldier, I need to keep my focus on God and follow His commands. That sounds hard but I need to remember Jesus lives within me via the Holy Spirit, so I need to trust Him to guide, correct, and show me what to do. He will show me where I can be most effective.

One person does not have the power, strength, and resources to fix and help everyone, but God has **all** the power, strength, and resources. God has the plan; I'm going to trust and follow Him.

Heavenly Father, help me to cease striving and know that You are God. Help me to delight myself in You for the joy of the Lord is my strength. As I trust and acknowledge You, You will direct my paths. Thank You that nothing is impossible for You, Your unfailing love will guide us, for You know the plans for each of us. I love You, Father! (Psalm 46:10, Psalm 37:4, Nehemiah 8:10, Proverbs 3:5-6, Luke 1:37, Exodus 15:13, Jeremiah 29:11)

Where the River flows

While studying the book of Ezekiel, I came upon this passage... "Now he brought me back to the entrance to the Temple. I saw water pouring out from under the Temple porch to the east (the Temple faced east). The water poured from the south side of the Temple, south of the altar. ... The water was gushing from under the south front of the Temple. ... **Wherever the river flows, life will flourish—** great schools of fish—because the river is turning the salt sea into fresh water. **Where the river flows, life abounds...** But the river itself, on both banks, will grow fruit trees of all kinds. Their leaves won't wither, the fruit won't fail. Every month they'll bear fresh fruit because the river from the Sanctuary flows to them. Their fruit will be for food and their leaves for healing." ~ Ezekiel 47: 1-2, 8, 12 (MSG) (bold mine)

Where the river flows from the temple... Where the river flows there is life, life flourishing and abounding, non-withering leaves on trees bearing fresh fruit to feed and heal.

Jesus is the Life, the Way, and the Truth. He came to bring us life, abundant abounding life. He is the living water that flows to us, in us, and out from us. Through Christ we never die, our souls flourish with His life. As we abide in the Lord, we bear His fruit that feeds and heals.

Where the living water flows is unending beauty.

As a Christian you can allow His river to flow in you and through you to nourish, flourish, and bless!

Heavenly Father, thank You for Your Son, Jesus who gifts us with grace, mercy, and eternal life. Thank You that through Him we have abundant, flourishing, living-water life. Thank You! Help me abide in You, trust in You, so that Your living water always flows free.

"He who believes in Me, as the Scripture said, 'From his innermost being will flow rivers of living water.'... I came that they may have life and have it abundantly." ~ John 7:38, John 10:10 (NASB)

"I am the vine, you are the branches; he who abides in Me and I in him, he bears much fruit, for apart from Me you can do nothing." ~ John 15:5 (NASB)

"Or do you not know that your body is a temple of the Holy Spirit who is in you, whom you have from God, and that you are not your own?" ~ 1 Corinthians 6:19 (NASB)

"Blessed is the man who trusts in the Lord and whose trust is the Lord. For he will be like a tree planted by the water, that extends its roots by a stream and will not fear when the heat comes; but its leaves will be green, and it will not be anxious in a year of drought nor cease to yield fruit." ~ Jeremiah 17:7-8 (NASB)

Self-Expenditure

I have held various jobs in the workforce. Everywhere I worked, I was given a paycheck at the end of a certain timeframe. I was expected to work, and I expected to receive compensation for my work.

When God calls us to do something, it's easy to think in human terms there will be reward for our service. While that's true, the payment may not be received here on earth. God's plans and ways are much bigger than we can see with earthly eyes. We are created by an eternal God for eternal purposes.

As Christ followers, we are to spread His good news and share with others the hope and joy we have found through the mercy and grace of Jesus Christ. God gives and blesses so we can give and bless others. Living lives for Christ means abandoning our plans and our ways, releasing what He has given us for His kingdom.

One day I was unsettled and wondered if I was missing something. Oswald Chambers' devotion, *The Sacrament of Sacrifice*, waited in my inbox.

God's "...purpose is not the development of a man; His purpose is to make a man exactly like Himself, and the characteristic of the Son of God is self-expenditure. If we believe in Jesus, it is not what we gain, but what He pours through us that counts. ... Spiritually, we cannot measure our life by success, but only by what God pours through us, and we cannot measure that at all." ~ Oswald Chambers

Eureka! Revelation.

It's not what I gain in an earthly sense, but what's poured through me that counts. The self-expenditure of giving our all to Christ is so He can live His all in us and through us. "He must increase, but I must decrease." ~ John 3:30 (NKJV)

Like the story of the man who found a great and beautiful pearl and sold everything to make that purchase (see Matthew 13:45-46), giving all we have to Christ, who gave His all for us, gifts us with eternal life. As His life flows freely through our lives, our lives are changed and the ripple effects last for eternity.

Oh my, life is so much bigger than I imagine. I'm so limited by earthly thinking I often don't dare big dreams. I want to allow the Lord to completely use me for His perfect Kingdom purposes.

Oh Father, forgive me for looking for earthly blessings. I know I miss so much of what You are doing. Please forgive me. Help me to focus on Your kingdom, seek You above all, so that Your blessings flow in me and through me to be a blessing. Open my eyes to see how You are working. Open my ears to hear Your soft whispers in my soul so that I can always follow You. Flow in me and through Me for Your glory.

He is Near

Some virus thing made me weak, congested, and coughy. Wheeze... snort... hack... I don't know about you, but when my body is weak that's when the enemy seems to attack the most. I pictured myself growing older, older, older so much older, until I was alone, weak and helpless.

Whimper...

I picked up my Bible and noticed a beautiful phrase tucked between two popular verses. "Rejoice in the Lord always; again, I will say, rejoice! Let your gentle spirit be known to all men. **The Lord is near**. Be anxious for nothing, but in everything by prayer and supplication with thanksgiving let your requests be made known to God." ~ Philippians 4:4-6 (NASB)

Did you notice the reason we can rejoice and not be anxious? At the end of verse five we are reminded the beautiful truth; **The Lord is near**.

My visual about getting older was frightening and depressing, but that picture didn't contain the rest of the story. Whatever may come, Jesus is near. I might be weak and helpless, but I'll never be alone. The Lord will always be near.

God is already there in the future because He is timeless.

Whatever provision is needed; God will and has already provided.

Whatever grace is needed; God will and has already provided.

Whatever strength is needed; God will and has already provided.

Whatever visual you may see in your future, make sure you visualize Jesus with you in that future. He is near. He will never leave you or forsake you and will always be with you.

Rejoice friends, the Lord is near. Don't be anxious, the Lord is near. Praise the Lord, He is near!

"The Lord is near. Be anxious for nothing, but in everything by prayer and supplication with thanksgiving let your requests be made known to God." ~ Philippians 4:5b-6 (NASB)

Ashamed

Tears flowed down her checks; her head dropped in shame. Another held her baby, the child of her captor, the one who had stolen her innocence. Entire villages were pillaged. Women attacked, girls stolen, and now babies born from victimization. The women say their lives are over, that all hope is gone because of their shame.

My heart breaks for the heartbreak. I'm so angry at the injustice and the evil of men. The world is full of men, women, boys, and girls who have been victimized and attacked. Then the enemy plants lies that those victimized are the ones who should be ashamed. THAT IS A LIE! Satan is a liar -- that is who he is and what he does. Don't allow the enemy to rewrite the truth of God.

Oh, how I want to tell them (and tell you) there is nothing someone has done to you or that you have done that can separate you from the love of Christ.

You do NOT have to feel ashamed for what someone else did to you. You do not have to live in shame. There is no condemnation in Christ Jesus.

Take your shame to Jesus. Jesus took on our sin and shame, nailed it to the cross, conquered death and rose again so we don't live in sin and shame. You are free in Christ.

The enemy tries to tell you that you have been defiled and dishonored, but Jesus said, "Whatever comes from [the heart of] a man, that is what defiles and dishonors him." ~ Mark 7:20 (AMP)

I understand those emotions. I've been molested, raped, stalked, attacked, drugged and locked up. I've had some really rotten things happen to me, and the enemy tried to mess with my life and mess with my head. But God is a restoring, redeeming God.

Take what the enemy has used to try and shame you, throw back on his slimy head by living for Christ. Hurt the enemy for hurting you by living free in Christ and telling others how to live free in Christ.

Take what the enemy meant to destroy you, to use to destroy the enemy!

Oh, how I want to love on the women who have given birth to the child of their captors. Oh, how I want to encourage them to raise their children up for Christ to be spiritual warriors for Christ.

Raise your head, sweet one. Raise up the children to know and love their true Father God. Raise up in the truth that you are forever loved by Jesus Christ.

God is a Father to the fatherless, He is the One who sets the captives free, and He is the One who will never leave you or forsake you.

God takes your shame, washes you clean, restores your innocence, and gives you a new life and a new hope. Life free in the freedom of Christ.

Oh remember, please always remember, you are free and freely loved forever in Christ!

"I sought the Lord, and He answered me, and delivered me from all my fears. They looked to Him and were radiant, and their faces will never be ashamed." ~ Psalm 34:4-5 (NASB)

"Therefore, there is now no condemnation [no guilty verdict, no punishment] for those who are in Christ Jesus [who believe in Him as personal Lord and Savior]." ~ Romans 8:1 (AMP)

Let go!

He stood rigid, little fists clenched tight, face scrunched in disgust and shock – how dare his mommy want the bug. It was his! He had found it all by himself as he crawled on the patio, and that slimy critter just begged to be in his mouth. Fortunately, after a strong-willed battle, little Johnny's mom was able to wrestle the creepy-crawly from the toddler's hands.

Have you ever tried to get something from a small child they shouldn't have? Perhaps they pick up something harmful, or maybe they have something you want them to release so you can give them something better. Goodness, little hands can be very, very strong when the will is strong.

I am often just like that little boy, I clench something tight thinking it's what I need or must have, and **I don't want to let go**.

I've battled with God for years over some things I honestly thought were good things. However, I'm finding that even if the things are "good" in our eyes, it doesn't mean it's the best.

God doesn't want only the good, He wants the best. God knows us, completely knows us. He knows the past, present, and future. When God beckons us to let go, He is offering freedom. If what we are holding in our hands, or hearts, is blocking His best, we need to let go to receive His best.

Amazing freedom comes when we release everything to God.

When our hands (and hearts) are fully open to God, we are blessed with the bountiful blessings of God.

I want to let go of anything that isn't God's best. Heavenly Father, pry open my fingers and pry open my heart to be fully and completely open to You. Help me to let go to receive Your perfect will and Your perfect best.

"Open up before God, keep nothing back; he'll do whatever needs to be done." ~ Psalm 37:5 (MSG)

Thinking of you

Our Father leans close and whispers...

I am with you. I'll watch over you wherever you go. My love for you is unfailing. I won't ever leave or forsake you. I, your God, have a firm grip on you and I'm not letting go. I'm telling you don't panic. I'm right here to help you.

I delight in you. I will calm all your fears. I rejoice over you with joyful songs.

I love you so much I sent my Son, Jesus Christ, to pay the price for your sin.

Don't be afraid, I've redeemed you. I've called your name. You are mine. When you're in over your head, I'll be there with you. When you're in rough waters, you will not go down. When you're between a rock and a hard place, it won't be a dead end— Because I am God, your personal God, The Holy of Israel, your Savior. I paid a huge price for you.

Jesus will return to bring you home where a place has been prepared for you. And I will wipe the tears from your eyes. There won't be any more death, mourning, or pain. You'll drink freely of the living water, and you will be my sons and daughters, and I will be your God.

Please don't ever forget how much I love you!

(Genesis 28:15 NIV, Psalm 147:11 NIV, Joshua 1:5 NIV, Isaiah 41:13-14 MSG, Zephaniah 3:17 NLT, John 3:16 NIV, Isaiah 43:2-4 MSG, John 14:3 NIV, Revelation 7:17, 21:4, 6-7 NIV).

Spring the trap!

"If you forgive those who sin against you, your heavenly Father will forgive you. But if you refuse to forgive others, your Father will not forgive your sins."
~ Matthew 6:14-15 (NLT)

Forgiving the ones who hurt us, harmed us, or hurt or harmed our loved ones is difficult. Forgiving someone who did wrong almost seems wrong. The world, and especially Satan, tells us surely a loving God wouldn't want us to forgive "that" person. Satan's lie is you are losing when you forgive -- you lose and your nemesis wins. It's not true. Satan is a liar.

Unforgiveness is not your friend.

Does unforgiveness help you sleep at night?

Does unforgiveness help you feel good about life, about the past or the future?

Does unforgiveness help you with your current relationships?

Does unforgiveness make you a better person?

Does unforgiveness work for you or work against you?

Unforgiveness is not your friend!

When you don't forgive, unforgiveness eats at you from the inside out; it eats at you and eats at your relationships. Unforgiveness is Satan's weapon to destroy you and everyone around you.

Forgiving others springs you from Satan's trap.

Forgiveness isn't a gift to the other person; forgiveness is a gift to you.

Forgiving others cuts the tie with that person, that circumstance, those people, and that situation.

Forgiveness frees you. Forgiveness releases you and gifts you with God's forgiveness. Forgiving others frees you to sleep at night to have a life now and in the future. Forgiving others frees you to live again.

Jesus said, forgive and you will be forgiven. Forgiveness isn't about the other person and what they did, it's about you. Forgiveness isn't a gift to the one who harmed you; forgiving others is a gift for yourself.

The truth sets you free. When you forgive, you open God's conduit for forgiveness for you, you open the conduit for His blessings and a renewed relationship with Him and others.

Forgiving others is the key to your freedom. Spring free of Satan's trap. Right now, this moment, experience your freedom by forgiving them.

Heavenly Father, I don't like what they did to me. It was wrong and it was so very painful. Forgiving them is so very hard, but Father I want to be free, so Father I forgive them. I trust You to do what is right even if I can't see You working. I will trust that You will hold them accountable for their actions. I release them to You so that I can be free!

Our Crazy Times

I woke in the middle of the night concerned about our country. Our world is a mess and sometimes I let the craziness get to me. Fortunately, scriptural truth came to mind as I pondered the situation.

These truths helped me, and I pray they also help you.

Pray for those in office and in authority. "The first thing I want you to do is pray. Pray every way you know how, for everyone you know. Pray especially for rulers and their governments to rule well so we can be quietly about our business of living simply, in humble contemplation. This is the way our Savior God wants us to live." ~ 1 Timothy 2:1-3 (MSG)

Ask for wisdom. "If any of you lacks wisdom [to guide him through a decision or circumstance], he is to ask of [our benevolent] God, who gives to everyone generously and without rebuke or blame, and it will be given to him." ~ James 1:5 (AMP)

Don't be anxious. "Be anxious for nothing, but in everything by prayer and supplication with thanksgiving let your requests be made known to God." ~ Philippians 4:6 (NASB)

Don't be afraid. "Be strong and courageous, do not be afraid or tremble at them, for the Lord your God is the one who goes with you. He will not fail you or forsake you... "These things I have spoken to you, so that in Me you may have peace. In the world you have tribulation but take courage; I have overcome the world. For whatever is born of God overcomes the world; and this is the victory that has overcome the world—our faith." ~ Deuteronomy 31:6 (NASB), John 16:33 (NASB) 1 John 5:4 (NASB)

Keep your perspective. "So, if you're serious about living this new resurrection life with Christ, act like it. Pursue the things over which Christ presides. Don't shuffle along, eyes to the ground, absorbed with the things right in front of you. Look up and be alert to what is going on around Christ—that's where the action is. See things from his perspective." ~ Colossians 3:1-2 (MSG)

Walk the talk. "...walk in a manner worthy of the calling with which you have been called, with all humility and gentleness, with patience, showing tolerance for one another in love, being diligent to preserve the unity of the Spirit in the bond of peace. Let your gentle spirit be known to all men. The Lord is near. Be anxious for nothing, but in everything by prayer and supplication with thanksgiving let your requests be made known to God. And the peace of God, which surpasses all comprehension, will guard your hearts and your minds in Christ Jesus. Above all, keep fervent in your love for one another, because love covers a multitude of sins." ~ Ephesians 4:1-3 (NASB), Philippians 4:5-7 (NASB), 1 Peter 4:8 (NASB)

Remember we aren't fighting one another. "For our struggle is not against flesh and blood, but against the rulers, against the powers, against the world forces of this darkness, against the spiritual forces of wickedness in the heavenly places." ~ Ephesians 6:12 (NASB)

Don't try to take matters in your own hands. "Do not be overcome by evil but overcome evil with good. Never take your own revenge, beloved, but leave room for the wrath of God, for it is written, 'Vengeance is Mine, I will repay,' says the Lord." ~ Romans 12:21 (NASB), Romans 12:19 (NASB)

Live in peace. "Cease striving and know that I am God; I will be exalted among the nations; I will be exalted in the earth. If it is possible, as far as it depends on you, live at peace with everyone. Let the peace of Christ rule in your hearts, to which indeed you were called in one body; and be thankful. For He Himself is our peace.... Peace I leave with you; My peace I give to you; not as the world gives do I give to you. Do not let your heart be troubled, nor let it be fearful." ~ Psalm 46:10 (NASB), Romans 12:18 (NIV), Colossians 3:15 (NASB), Ephesians 2:14 (NASB), John 14:27 (NASB)

Stand firm and keep on your armor. "Put on the full armor of God, so that you will be able to stand firm against the schemes of the devil." ~ Ephesians 6:11 (NASB)

Stay on mission. "Go therefore and make disciples of all the nations, baptizing them in the name of the Father and the Son and the Holy Spirit, teaching them to observe all that I commanded you; and lo, I am with you always, even to the end of the age." ~ Matthew 28:19-20 (NASB)

Always remember God is in control. "For the kingdom is the Lord's and He rules over the nations. He rules by His might forever; His eyes keep watch on the nations; let not the rebellious exalt themselves.

The Lord has established His throne in the heavens, and His sovereignty rules over all." ~ Psalm 22:28 (NASB), Psalm 66:7 (NASB), Psalm 103:19 (NASB)

And no matter how crazy it gets, always remember "nothing will be impossible with God." ~ Luke 1:37 (NASB)

Listening and watching

As a writer, I know every word matters and each one should have a purpose. Every word spoken or written can impact and imprint someone's life.

Throughout the Bible, people heard of God and Jesus. Those who listened were drawn to God's love.

"**When she heard** in Moab that the LORD had come to the aid of his people by providing food for them, Naomi and her daughters-in-law prepared to return home from there." ~ Ruth 1:6 (NIV)

"Two blind men were sitting by the roadside, and **when they heard** that Jesus was going by, they shouted, 'Lord, Son of David, have mercy on us!'" (Matthew 20:30 NIV).

"**When they heard** all he was doing, many people came to him from Judea, Jerusalem, Idumea, and the regions across the Jordan and around Tyre and Sidon." ~ Mark 3:8 (NIV)

"**When she heard** about Jesus, she came up behind him in the crowd and touched his cloak." ~ Mark 5:27 (NIV).

"In fact, as soon as **she heard** about him, a woman whose little daughter was possessed by an evil spirit came and fell at his feet." ~ Mark 7:25 (NIV)

"A few days later, when Jesus again entered Capernaum, **the people heard** that he had come home. Some men came, bringing to him a paralytic, carried by four of them... ~ Mark 2:1,3-4 (NIV).

My question for us all....

Do our words bring people to Jesus?

How far will we go to bring others to Him?

How willing are we to help those in need?

People are listening and watching, what do your actions and words say?

Heavenly Father please help me be aware of my thoughts, actions, and words so that anyone watching or listening will be drawn to You.

Loaded Up

Have you ever helped a child prepare for their morning at school? Not wanting our little ones to be without what they need, we make sure their backpack has the daily provision – lunch or lunch money, books, paper, pens, pencils, homework, permission slips, maybe a Band-Aid or two for any bumps or bruises, a note for encouragement, etc...

Every day there are requirements for that day, and every day we check to make sure they have what they need.

Did you know before you were born, your Heavenly Father knew what you would need for every single one of your days?

I chuckled this morning as I pictured angels before I was birthed into this world loading up my "backpack" for my life journey. Perhaps a heavenly conveyor-belt filled with God's word, His truth, financial provision, the writings of saints before me, soul-wound bandages, grace notes, wisdom, the fruit of the Spirit.... Everything loaded up and pre-prepared.

Whatever we face, God's provision is already provided. Nothing is forgotten or overlooked because God knows every breath we take and every need we need.

Rest easy, friends. God's provision is already loaded up!

"His divine power has given us everything we need for a godly life through our knowledge of him who called us by his own glory and goodness." ~ 2 Peter 1:3 (NIV)

"And God is able to bless you abundantly, so that in all things at all times, having all that you need you will abound in every good work." ~ 2 Corinthians 9:8 (NIV)

Unexpected

You know those unexpected moments, the ones that creep up on you and send your world reeling? Or the ones that body-slam you to the pavement out of left field.

Ack!

When it comes to negative life interruptions, I could list a list that would take years to list. Goodness, the world can be such a difficult place.

As I contemplated the news and prayer requests just from today, I felt like I could hyper-ventilate. It's... all... just... too... much.

Then I remembered, God's got this.

God's got this.

God's got that situation... that person... those people... that difficulty ... that heartache... that need. He never slumbers or sleeps, and His love is unfailing.

Remembering God has the world in His hands, nothing is impossible for Him, no need is too great for Him, and nothing happens that catches Him by surprise. Those truths give me air to breathe.

God has all the needs of our unexpected needs already expected and everything we need ready for what we will go through.

We may be surprised by the unexpected, but there are no surprises for The One who knows all. God's got this. Remember, God's got this.

Breathe, friend. ***God's got this.***

"Do not fear, for I am with you; do not anxiously look about you, for I am your God. I will strengthen you, surely I will help you, surely I will uphold you with My righteous right hand." ~ Isaiah 41:10 (NASB)

"Don't fret or worry. Instead of worrying, pray. Let petitions and praises shape your worries into prayers, letting God know your concerns. Before you know it, a sense of God's wholeness, everything coming together for good, will come and settle you down. It's wonderful what happens when Christ displaces worry at the center of your life." ~ Philippians 4:6-7 (MSG)

To be or not to be... I'm being for Him!

Does anyone else struggle with who they are supposed to be? I want to be the best me, but sometimes I'm not even sure who I'm really meant to be.

I'm a woman, wife, mom, Christian, author, friend, the list goes on and on, and trying to be the best in all those areas can sometimes drive me crazy. Goodness, trying to be the best in just one area can drive me nuts.

Psalm 46:10 comes to mind reminding me to be still, cease striving and know that God is God.

Whew.

God is God, and He is big enough to help me be what He wants me to be. Nothing is too hard for God, all things are possible for God, and He is faithful to complete what He starts.

So, it's not all about me. Really, it's not. Scary thought. Freeing thought. Amazingly freeing thought! God's in control and it's all about Him and pointing to Him. Woot! I'm free to be me in the beauty of God to point to the love and beauty of God.

I'm going to enjoy life not worrying about me being me, and instead being all about Him. Let's be the best we can be, by being in Christ!

I pray, "That you may really come to know [practically, through experience for yourselves] the love of Christ, which far surpasses mere knowledge [without experience]; that you may be filled [through all your being] unto all the fullness of God [may have the richest measure of the divine Presence, and become a body wholly filled and flooded with God Himself]!" ~ Ephesians 3:19 (AMPC)

"My whole being shall be satisfied ... and my mouth shall praise You with joyful lips. My whole being follows hard after You and clings closely to You; Your right hand upholds me." ~ Psalm 63:5 (AMPC), Psalm 63:8 (AMPC)

They didn't waste the gift

Before our son left for his job in Japan, we took him clothes shopping. He needed business suits, and since he is 6' 7", that isn't an easy task. He hated going shopping because of the difficulty finding something to fit his slender, tall frame.

We arrived at a men's clothing store and were greeted by a beautiful young woman named Carlie. She made us feel welcome, brought suits for him to try. and our son hesitantly obliged by taking them into the changing room. When Scott came out, he came out a different man. He looked great! He was thrilled to have something that looked good and actually fit.

Carlie was wonderful as she helped him find suits, shirts, ties, and even pocket squares. The time we spent with her was a delight for our whole family. She and our son talked about Japan and how she and her husband had thought about one day visiting that country. I tell ya, we were tearing up by the time we left as God had answered prayers in getting our son ready for his big trip.

Because Scott so enjoyed Carlie, he ordered books that taught Japanese to share with her and her husband. She was very touched by his thoughtfulness. And the cool thing is, Carlie and her husband used the books and now can write and read a little Japanese.

Scott was thrilled to hear of their progress, and it blessed my heart to see how he shared and gave me great joy to see how the gifts were used.

One thing it made me realize is when God gifts us with something, when we enjoy them, use them for His glory, I'm sure that blesses Him with joy.

God blesses each of us with gifts. However, we have a choice how (and if) we will use what He gives us. His gifts are meant to be used. The illustration given by Jesus in Matthew 25:14-30 reminds us to be diligent to use the gifts we are given.

The servants who used their master's gifts were blessed. "His lord said to him, 'Well done, good and faithful servant; you were faithful over a few things, I will make you ruler over many things. Enter into the joy of your lord.'" ~ Matthew 25:21 (NKJV) The servant who did not use his gift, lost the gift and was punished.

I don't want to lose my gift and I sure don't want to lose the joy of my Master. I want to enter into the joy of my Lord! I believe I've been gifted and called to write; therefore, I need to keep writing. As I use His gift for His glory, I believe I'm bringing Him joy which gives me joy. Woot! Joy party for us all!

What gifts has the Lord given you? Are you using your gifting? Please don't miss the joy because joy comes for the faithful servant.

"God has given each of you a gift from his great variety of spiritual gifts. Use them well to serve one another." ~ 1 Peter 4:10 (NLT)

"Since we have gifts that differ according to the grace given to us each of us is to exercise them accordingly: if prophecy, according to the proportion of his faith; if service, in his serving; or he who teaches, in his teaching; or he who exhorts, in his exhortation; he who gives, with liberality; he who leads, with diligence; he who shows mercy, with cheerfulness." ~ Romans 12:6-8 (NASB)

"Now there are varieties of gifts, but the same Spirit. And there are varieties of ministries, and the same Lord. There are varieties of effects, but the same God who works all things in all persons." ~ 1 Corinthians 12:4-6 (NASB)

Shine like the Son

I awakened to the worries of the world. So much evil, so many difficulties, racial tension, political issues, people issues, and the news reporting every bit of bad news they can find. Frustration set in as I thought how the media distorts and manipulates, leaning their reports to meet their agendas.

I looked out the window and through the trees a golden glow illuminated the morning sky. I watched awestruck and blessed as the glory of the Lord colored the heavens. Oh yes, God is still in control. Oh yes, good things are happening as the Lord continues to work. God is great, mighty, powerful, and glorious.

The world is darkening, but God's light is never dimmed, and for those of us who have Christ in our hearts, His light will always shine.

Oh, let's shine like the SON. Let's allow our lights to shine. Let's illuminate the earth and the sky with the glory of the Lord.

Report the good news to the world and shine the light of Christ. Can you imagine if we all truly shined our SON lights? The world would be illuminated with the beauty and truth of God's love.

Shine, shine, shine, shine like the SON!

"Let your light shine before men in such a way that they may see your good works and glorify your Father who is in heaven." ~ Matthew 5:16 (NASB)

"... the path of the righteous is like the light of dawn, that **shines brighter and brighter** until the full day." ~ Proverbs 4:18 (NASB)

"The people who walk in darkness will see a great light; those who live in a dark land, **the light will shine** on them." ~ Isaiah 9:2 (NASB)

"**Arise, shine**; for your light has come, and the glory of **the Lord has risen upon yo**u. For behold, darkness will cover the earth and deep darkness the peoples; but the Lord will rise upon you and **His glory will appear upon you.**" ~ Isaiah 60:1-2 (NASB) (Emphasis added)

Restricted

"...Restricted by your own affections." ~ 2 Corinthians 6:12 (NKJV) I read the verse and wondered how often earthly affections get in the way of heavenly pursuits.

Do worries overrule joy?

Does the list of wants and wishes overshadow God-given blessings?

Does resentment and demands on time by family and friends eclipse the embodied gift of each person?

Is the pursuit of our own affections keeping us from seeing, enjoying, and experiencing God's abundance?

Would you be willing to pray with me?

Heavenly Father help me to pursue You above any earthly desire. Help me never to allow my affections for anyone or anything to restrict You. Help my joy of You overrule my worry.

Help me notice Your blessings more than my wants and wishes. Help me to see the giftings You have placed in each friend and family member. And please help my affection for You be above all so that I can see enjoy and experience Your amazing abundance. Unrestrict my restrictions to be completely unrestricted in Your love!

Smoking and shaking

Several years ago, my husband and I spent a quiet afternoon shopping. Our lazy wanderings were interrupted when my cell phone rang.

"Lisa," my mom's voice struggled to remain calm, "your security company just called. Your fire alarm is going off and the fire department is on their way."

My husband and I hurried to the car and prayed all the way home. We were so grateful our smoke detectors were hard-wired in case of trouble to automatically notify the fire department.

When we arrived, neighbors were gathered on the street and fire-fighters were already positioned to enter by force. House alarms screeching, we hurried and unlocked the door. Smoke and a nauseous odor billowed out. Our poor little dog, wide-eyed and shaking so much I thought his fur would fly off, ran to our waiting arms.

Fire-fighters rushed inside. We waited and prayed. Within minutes, the source of the smoke was found. A tea kettle had been left on a burner. What remained was a partially molten mass only seconds away from igniting.

Besides a traumatized dog, a destroyed kettle, and a horrible odor, everything was fine.

However, if not for the fire and smoke alarms, our situation would have ended in disaster. Warnings have a purpose—protection and a chance for escape.

The world is smoking and shaking, and God is calling. Please don't miss the warnings. Please don't wait.

Heaven is real and so is hell.

Jesus is The Rescue, The Way, the Escape. Through Him we have forgiveness and eternal life. Jesus is the key to heaven and eternal freedom.

God allows us to choose Heaven by accepting His Son, Jesus Christ as Savior.

Or we have another choice. We can say no. We can turn our back on God.

Both choices have eternal consequences. The warning is for your benefit. Please don't ignore the warnings. Don't miss your chance. Please don't miss your chance.

The world is shaking and smoking with warning signs. Time is short. God is calling. Choose heaven by choosing God's Son, Jesus Christ.

"For God so loved the world that he gave his one and only Son, that whoever believes in him shall not perish but have eternal life. For God did not send his Son into the world to condemn the world, but to save the world through him.

Jesus answered, 'I am the way and the truth and the life. No one comes to the Father except through me. Come to Me, all who are weary and heavy-laden, and I will give you rest.' For the wages of sin is death, but the free gift of God is eternal life in Christ Jesus our Lord....

"If you confess with your mouth Jesus as Lord and believe in your heart that God raised Him from the dead, you will be saved; for with the heart a person believes, resulting in righteousness, and with the mouth he confesses, resulting in salvation. For whoever calls on the name of the Lord shall be saved. So, if the Son makes you free, you will be free indeed." ~ John 3:16-17, John 14:6 (NIV). Matthew 11:28 (NASB), Romans 6:23 (NASB), Romans 10:9-10 (NASB), Romans 10:13 (NKJV) John 8:36 (NASB)

Pronouncing Sentence

I wonder ... does our sentence, pronounce a sentence? If I say, "I feel bad." Will my body react negatively? By saying, "I feel good." Will my body react by feeling better?

The Bible tells us our words matter, that life and death are in the tongue (Proverbs 18:21).

Words have an impact and reverberates in our souls.

Words propel or hinder.

Words motivate or discourage.

Words bring freedom or imprisonment.

Harsh words make tempers flare (Proverbs 15:1).

Flattering words bring ruin (Proverbs 26:28).

Kind words are like honey—sweet to the soul and healthy for the body (Proverbs 16:24).

Gentle words are a tree of life (Proverbs 15:4).

Praise words bring us closer to God (Psalm 100:4).

Our thoughts and our words affect our hearts and the hearts of others. Let's be careful to control our sentences by bringing our sentences under control of The One who is the Word who spoke life into existence.

Let's pronounce sentence over our sentences by controlling our sentences to pronounce life, peace, and joy by speaking of The One who is life, peace, and joy.

Let's sentence our bodies to the goodness of The One who is good.

Regardless of how our body may feel or what we may be going through, we can fully live in the goodness of The One who is good.

What sentences will you speak?

Heavenly Father, please help me control what I say to others and what I say to myself. Please help my sentences be pleasing to You. And, "may the words of my mouth and the meditation of my heart be pleasing to you, O Lord, my rock and my redeemer." ~ Psalm 19:14 (NLT)

Revival

As I prayed for revival, I wondered if my request was because I want everything in our country and world to be "good"? Am I asking for revival so life can be pleasing to me?

James wrote, "...even when you ask, you don't get it because your motives are all wrong—you want only what will give you pleasure." ~ James 4:3 (NLT)

I need to rethink what I'm thinking and re-pray what I'm praying. I need to seek revival in order that lives can be saved for eternity. I need to ask for revival so that I and others are driven deeper into God's heart.

Heavenly Father, I humbly ask for revival. Revive me to grow deeper in You. Revive me to live with full abandonment in Your perfect will. Revive our county to turn back to You, to seek You, to love You with our whole hearts, body, mind, soul, and strength. Help us to love You enough to speak Your truth. Help us to love You enough to walk in Your ways. Help us to love You enough to read and know Your Word. Revive us to spark a revival that ignites the world for You!

"For thus says the One who is high and lifted up, who inhabits eternity, whose name is Holy: I dwell in the high and holy place, and also with him who is of a contrite and lowly spirit, to revive the spirit of the lowly, and to revive the heart of the contrite." ~ Isaiah 57:15 (ESV)

"If My people who are called by My name will humble themselves, and pray and seek My face, and turn from their wicked ways, then I will hear from heaven, and will forgive their sin and heal their land."
~ 2 Chronicles 7:14 (NKJV)

Cross-Time Race

Have you ever watched a cross-country race? Runners gather at the starting line and people cheer and encourage the contestants. However, as the journey lengthens, the well-wishers decrease and are only sporadic. Perhaps there will be a few refreshing stations along the way to rehydrate and reenergize, but companionship is virtually non-existent.

The pack of runners stretches out as the strong pass the weak. There are mountains to climb, deserts to cross, and the way gets lonelier and more difficult.

Competitors have countless motivations for running. Some want the cool t-shirt or bragging rights, others run to prove something to themselves or others. There are the few, those who run to win the prize, who won't give up, and won't stop for they are determined to win.

As Christians we are in a Cross-Time Race. We run in the grace-shadow of the cross. Smooth roads with cheering crowds would be preferred, but the way has hardships to endure and trials to encounter. Deserts come and mountains rise in front of us, and often encouragers are no longer there to encourage.

Life is a moving journey. People come and go, and many times we'll feel alone. It's tempting to want to return to the starting line for support, but if we do, we won't ever move forward. Or if we refuse to leave the place that refreshed us the most, we will miss the rest of the amazing journey.

Don't give up, don't lose hope, and don't lose the perspective to press on.

Press on to reach the end of the race and receive the heavenly prize for which God, through Christ Jesus, is calling you.

Press on friends and run the race to win!

"...Forgetting the past and looking forward to what lies ahead, I press on to reach the end of the race and receive the heavenly prize for which God, through Christ Jesus, is calling us. Don't you realize that in a race everyone runs, but only one person gets the prize? So, run to win!" ~ Philippians 3:13-14, 1 Corinthians 9:24 (NLT)

Needing Rest

Life is so unsettled. Everyone seems restless. Or maybe it's just me. Ugh. Between the media and unsettling news at home, I've been restless.

Yes, I know God is in control. I really know that, but goodness it's hard not knowing what's coming next. I want to plan, and have an idea on what to do, where to go, who to be, and how to be the best woman God created me to be.

And then I read this verse... "For thus said the Lord God, the Holy One of Israel, 'In **returning and rest** you shall be saved; in **quietness** and in **trust** shall be your strength.'" ~ Isaiah 30:15 (ESV) (my highlights)

Return. Rest in quietness. Trust.

Relieved sigh...

Oh, Heavenly Father, I've been so restless and so very unsettled. Please forgive me. Thank You for Your word that beckons us to come to You. I don't need to know the future, I don't need to analyze the possibilities, I just need to rest at Your feet. Help me to return to You, rest in the quietness of You, and trust You. Thank You, Father. I'm laying down my soul in Your strong arms. I love You.

Looking for Hope

I want hope, and sometimes I'm not sure where my hope went. Yes, I can give you a list of excuses and they are all legitimate. I'm embarrassed by this revelation. I'm a Christian so I'm really never without hope. I know that in my head. I know that truth in my heart. I have eternal hope.

Hope is given, a blessing, and an incredible, awesome truth. Hope exists and is an eternal, unfailing, wonderful gift from our Heavenly Father through His Son, Jesus Christ.

Unfortunately, on the flip side, we live in a fallen world with pain, hurt, and difficulties that are really painful, hurtful, and difficult. Life doesn't always turn out like we planned, and hope is sometimes shattered and fractured.

Hopelessness exists, but it's rooted in lies. Hopelessness says that hope is useless.

Hopelessness is a stalker that creeps in at the saddest, toughest times.

Hopelessness wants us to focus on the negative, the utter defeat of a situation, instead of turning to look at The One who defeated sin and death, Who finds nothing impossible.

Hopelessness wants us to look at that one thing, that one person, that one situation, so that we will miss the things God is doing, the people He is sending our way, the situations He is orchestrating to help us grow closer to Him.

Please remember, people will fail and fall away, circumstances are ever-changing, but God is constant. He is hope that never fails.

God does things beyond the time space continuum. God has no restrictions that restrict man. God provides, He heals, He restores, and He raises the dead to life. Nothing is too hard for Him. Nothing is impossible for God.

If hopelessness has crept into your life, turn to The One who is eternal hope.

"Why am I so sad? Why am I so upset? I should put my hope in God and keep praising Him, my Savior and my God. Lead me by Your truth and teach me, for You are the God who saves me. All day long I put my hope in You. Let Your unfailing love surround us, LORD, for our hope is in You alone.

"Wait and hope for and expect the Lord; be brave and of good courage and let your heart be stout and enduring. Yes, wait for and hope for and expect the Lord. So be strong and courageous, all you who put your hope in the LORD! The Lord looks after those who fear him, those who put their hope in his love.

"And so, Lord, where do I put my hope? My only hope is in you. I find rest in God; only He gives me hope. You are my refuge and my shield; Your word is my source of hope. I am counting on the LORD; yes, I am counting on him. I have put my hope in His word.

"Those who wait for the Lord [who expect, look for, and hope in Him] shall change and renew their strength and power; they shall lift their wings and mount up [close to God] as eagles [mount up to the sun]; they shall run and not be weary, they shall walk and not faint or become tired. 'For I know the plans I have for you,' says the LORD. 'They are plans for good and not for disaster, to give you a future and a hope.'"

Psalm 42:5 (NCV), Psalm 25:5 (NLT), Psalm 33:22 (NLT), Psalm 27:14 (AMP), Psalm 31:24 (NLT), Psalm 33:18 (NCV), Psalm 39:7 (NLT), Psalm 62:5 (NCV), Psalm 119:114 (NLT), Psalm 130:5 (NLT), Isaiah 40:31 (AMP), Jeremiah 29:11 (NLT)

Soul Contractor

I enjoy watching television shows where builders and renovators fix older homes. Regardless of the many problems a house may have, one contractor would come with his crew and always "make it right." The foundation could be a mess, the roof caving in, the plumbing and electrical a jumble of wires and pipes, but nothing would be too difficult for our hero contractor.

Jesus Christ is a soul contractor. No matter how messy our lives may be, nothing is too hard for our Savior.

When we come to Jesus, His grace, mercy, and forgiveness, sweeps through our lives renovating, restoring, and renewing. No job is too big or too small. His heroic, sacrificial, redeeming love restores all, and He always makes it right.

No matter how disheveled your life may look, remember that Jesus can always make it right!

"For no one can lay any foundation other than the one already laid, which is Jesus Christ. If anyone is in Christ, he is a new creation. The old has passed away, the new is here!" ~ 1 Corinthians 3:11, 2 Corinthians 5:17 (NIV)

Turn your eyes

Upset, mad and frustrated, all those emotions were making me crazy. I was angry, all-out furious at what is happening in our country and world. I'm mad that my friends are afraid. I'm mad at those who target the police because of the actions of some of the police. I'm mad that racism exists, and I'm mad at people and the media who fuel the fires of racism.

I had to get away from the media, away from the bad news, the heartache and pain. I went outside and mowed the yard. I needed to pray. To sweat. A 102-heat index provided the perspiration, and fortunately the Holy Spirit cooled me off with God's truth.

As I moved, I kept hearing the old hymn play in my head "Turn your yes upon Jesus."

Turn your eyes upon Jesus look full in His wonderful face and the things of earth will grow strangely dim in the light of His glory and grace. *

My anger melted away, and tears fell as I realized anger just adds anger and fear only adds more fear. Only the love of Jesus can extinguish anger and fear.

I'm praying for our country, praying for my friends and their families, praying for the police, for my friends of every color, and praying that we all will turn our eyes upon Jesus.

Would you join me in praying?

Heavenly Father, help us to turn our eyes upon You. You are the only hope for any of us. You are the Savior. You are the redeemer and restorer.

Oh, Father I pray for unity among Your children, that we would love one another with Your love.

Accept one another with the acceptance You give. Help us to encourage, comfort, and uplift one another. Thank You Father that You are always in control and You are mighty enough for any and every need. I'm turning my eyes back to You and trusting You.

"Be angry [at sin—at immorality, at injustice, at ungodly behavior], yet do not sin; do not let your anger [cause you shame, nor allow it to] last until the sun goes down. Set your mind on the things above, not on the things that are on earth. Comfort and encourage and strengthen your hearts [keeping them steadfast and on course] in every good work and word. Keeping your faith [leaning completely on God with absolute trust and confidence in His guidance] Be patient; strengthen your hearts [keep them energized and firmly committed to God], because the coming of the Lord is near. Keep yourselves in the love of God, waiting anxiously for the mercy of our Lord Jesus Christ to eternal life." ~ Ephesians 4:26 (AMP), Colossians 3:2 (NASB), 2 Thessalonians 2:17 (AMP), 1 Timothy 1:19 (AMP), James 5:8 (AMP), Jude 1:21 (NASB)

Turn Your Eyes upon Jesus by Helen H. Lemmel

No More

When Jesus came into people's lives, their lives changed. The blind received sight, the lame could walk, and the outcasts and sinners were welcomed home.

I'm so in love with Jesus and I so want you to know His love. No one is too broken, no one has gone too far, and no one is beyond His loving reach. Oh, how He loves you! Oh, how He wants the best for you. He doesn't want you trapped in a sin that separates you from His love.

When we are told not to sin, God is giving us a boundary not to confine but to free us from fear, shame, and regret.

Jesus healed a man who had been ill for thirty-eight years then said, "See, you have been made well. Sin **no more**, lest a worse thing come upon you." ~ John 5:14 (NKJV)

The woman caught in adultery brought to Jesus to be stoned, once her accusers left, Jesus said, "Go. From now on sin **no more**." ~ John 8:11 (NASB)

When Jesus told sinners to sin **no more**, He offered a beautiful invitation for freedom. Sin was never embraced. Sin was addressed, and the sinner given healing, hope, and a new beginning.

No matter how bad or deeply rooted a sin, nothing is impossible for God. His unlimited power can release anyone and set captives free.

As bonus blessing, God takes our "no more" and creates abundance. Faced with over 5000 people to feed, the disciples saw only their small provisions.

"We have **no more** than five loaves and two fish." Yet in the hands of Jesus, all were fed with over twelve baskets full of leftovers (Luke 9:12-17).

Jesus frees us from the worries of this life. "I say to you, my friends, do not be afraid of those who kill the body and after that have **no more** that they can do." ~ Luke 12:4 (NASB)

And in the end, for those who follow Jesus, we discover no more of the heartache and pain of this world. "And God will wipe away every tear from their eyes; there shall be no more death, nor sorrow, nor crying. There shall be **no more** pain, for the former things have passed away." ~ Revelation 21:4 (NKJV)

When you have Jesus in your life, **no more** do you have to live in sin, no more do you have to worry about provision, no more do you have the fear of man, and no more do you have to worry about your ending. Jesus sets you free to live in His eternal abundant joy!

Waste no more time in your sin, in your worry, or in your fears... run to Jesus, His loving arms are open wide!

Floundering

Watching the news or looking on social media bombards us with negativity, heartache, and pain. Goodness, can't we all just get along?

Then if occurred to me, the world reports on the world. And a world without God is hopeless, negative, and filled with heartache and pain.

Christians aren't immune to trouble. Jesus warned us we will have trouble, and boy the world is troublesome. I may at times be floundering, but I can stay solid on The Solid Rock of Jesus.

If I look to the world, I'll be troubled by the world. If I look to Jesus, I'll see beyond the world's troubles. Jesus is truth and The Truth sets me free. Jesus is life, hope, and peace. Jesus Christ is The Good News.

Let's tell others the Good News of Jesus Christ. Let's encourage one another by reporting what God is doing.

Heavenly Father, I've been floundering in all the negativity. Forgive me for focusing on the problems of the world more than the problem-solver of the world. Refocus my focus on You and Your love so that I may tell others of Your wonderful love. Thank You that in You we find hope, joy, and peace.

Jesus said, "trusting me, you will be unshakable and assured, deeply at peace. In this godless world you will continue to experience difficulties. But take heart! I've conquered the world." John 16:33 (MSG)

"Summing it all up, friends, I'd say you'll do best by filling your minds and meditating on things true, noble, reputable, authentic, compelling, gracious—the best, not the worst; the beautiful, not the ugly; things to praise, not things to curse. Put into practice what you learned from me, what you heard and saw and realized. Do that, and God, who makes everything work together, will work you into his most excellent harmonies." ~ Philippians 4:8-9 (MSG)

If today was my last day

If today was my last day...

I would want you to know that God loves you. I would want you to know His grace is available for you.

I would want you to know God is a God of grace, mercy, and love. God is also a God of justice --that person who wronged you, that got away with something very evil, God knows the truth and will repay.

I would want you to know that sometimes God's children don't always behave like God's children, and I'm sorry.

I would want you to know that sometimes people claim to be God's people, but they are not telling the truth. They lie.

I would want you to know that God is our Heavenly Father, a good, loving, Father. There is no evil in Him. He is kind, compassionate, gentle, pure love.

I would want you to know that hell exists. But God doesn't send people to hell, God lets us decide. We choose. We can choose to put our faith and trust in His Son, Jesus Christ who offers forgiveness for sins and a way to Heaven. Or we chose to turn away. Please don't risk choosing the wrong way.

If today was my last day, I would be waiting and hoping to see **you** in heaven.

"As the Scripture says, 'anyone who trusts in him will never be disappointed.' That Scripture says 'anyone' because there is no difference between those who are Jews and those who are not. The same Lord is the Lord of all and gives many blessings to all who trust in him, as the Scripture says, 'Anyone who calls on the Lord will be saved.'" ~ Romans 10:11-13 (NCV)

Tracking thoughts

God is teaching me again the beauty of taking every thought captive. Far too long I've had the tendency to analyze, wonder, and try to figure out when I hear something or see something and "go there" in my mind.

However, I've found I don't have to ponder every story, person's situation or hardship, or news report. I don't have to let my mind wander about my stuff or anyone else's stuff. The concerns of this world, of our families and friends, of our own lives, can and should be taken to God. He's the One with all the answers, the solutions, peace, comfort, hope and healing needed.

Thinking about something and praying about something are very different. I can think all day about problems, but when I pray about problems, then I've found the power from God to solve every problem.

I'm going to declutter the clutter of my mind by stopping any train of thought that leads to useless worry and fretting. Unless a thought brings me closer to God and His word, unless it uplifts, encourages, brings hope and light, I don't have to let it mess with my head and mess in my head. If the thought isn't a Godly thought, I can stop it in its tracks and throw it out.

Following after worthless thoughts lead to worthless thinking.

Perfect peace comes through keeping the mind focused on The One Who is perfect peace.

Instead of trying to figure out on my own, leaning on my own understanding, and thinking about every thought that comes my way, I need to take every thought to God. Godly wisdom comes from above, so I need to keep my thoughts trained on The One who is above.

When a thought comes, I'm checking which track that thought will lead. Will the thought track me to God or track me away from God?

Let's keep our thoughts on the right track by tracking them by God's truth.

"We demolish arguments and every pretension that sets itself up against the knowledge of God, and we take captive every thought to make it obedient to Christ." ~ 2 Corinthians 10:5 (NIV)

"Finally, brothers and sisters, whatever is true, whatever is noble, whatever is right, whatever is pure, whatever is lovely, whatever is admirable—if anything is excellent or praiseworthy—think about such things." ~ Philippians 4:8 (NIV)

Blazing

An icepick-to-the-head migraine woke me at night. I tried to get comfortable, attempted to get back to sleep, but then our elderly dog woke up and needed to go outside. I was hurting, tired, irritable, so very irritable and tired and hurting, and all I wanted to do was cry and try to sleep. However, once I was up, I decided to get moving, even if I really didn't want to move

I turned on the coffee pot and then trudged into my office. My gaze fell on a familiar verse - 2 Timothy 1:6 where Paul encouraged Timothy to kindle afresh, stir up, fan into flame, and keep ablaze the gift of God within him.

In my exhausted irritable soul, I felt a flicker, a rekindling. I read the words again, and realized we keep our faith fires burning by reading and memorizing God's word. Through Bible study and talking and sharing about God, our focus stays on God. We feed The Word within us with His Word.

Not only did Paul encourage Timothy to keep his fire burning, he reminded him of the reason to stay blazing for Christ. "Therefore, I remind you to stir up the gift of God which is in you through the laying on of my hands. **For God has not given us a spirit of fear, but of power and of love and of a sound mind.**" ~ 2 Timothy 1:6-7 (NKJV) (emphasis added.)

Our souls can stay ablaze for we have nothing to fear because fear is NOT from God. We have THE power of God.

We have THE unfailing, eternal love of our unfailing, eternal God. And we have a sound mind – THE mind of Christ is given to those who are in Christ (1 Corinthians 2:16).

Let's ignite our soul-fires back into flame by remembering God's truth. Fan the flames and keep blazing with the light of Christ, living fearless in His power and love!

"Therefore, I remind you to stir up the gift of God which is in you through the laying on of my hands. For God has not given us a spirit of fear, but of power and of love and of a sound mind." ~ 2 Timothy 1:6-7 (NKJV)

Specifically

Has someone asked you for prayer, and you prayed based on your understanding, then found out later the need was actually for something different?

I pray when others ask for general prayer. However, when the request is specific, I know how to specifically pray. Details are not needed; but clarity is appreciated.

I so appreciate one of our pastors, when someone came to him for prayer, he would ask specific questions to find out how they would like for him to pray.

God knows our every need and is never limited by our lack of communication skills or method of praying. I've had times all I could do was pray, "Help!" Thankfully, the Holy Spirit is there to translate every request.

Sometimes when I stumble through a prayer not sure really how to ask or what to ask, I take great comfort knowing the Holy Spirit is probably leaning over to God and saying, "This is what she means..."

I wonder if the times I throw up a prayer, or don't come to God with more than a vague request, will I see how God is working and answering?

If a request is specific, I know when He's specifically answered.

If I pray, "Please bless my friend" God's blessings may come (and will come) in various ways, but will I even notice the answers?

If my request takes on a more direct manner, "Please bless my friend _____ with the blessing of opening their heart to know You as Lord and Savior," I now have a tangible way to watch how God moves. By drilling down to understand what we are asking, we know better the true need and then later can see the ways God answers.

When you are able, ask specifically, record your request, and you too will be able to see the amazing ways God leads, provides, comforts, and works in your life and the lives of others.

"Be anxious for nothing, but in everything by prayer and supplication with thanksgiving let your requests be made known to God." ~ Philippians 4:6 (NASB)

Through it all

Astigmatism and extreme nearsightedness have been a challenge since childhood. I am so grateful for corrective lenses. Oh, my goodness, what a blessing.

After my last eye exam, I was sent to a specialist. During the marathon exam they found several issues — macular degeneration in both eyes, an epiretinal membrane on one eye (kind of like a piece of cellophane stuck on my retina making the world a little cloudy), an enlarged optic nerve in both eyes, growing drusens (multiple, small, round, yellow-white spots on the retina), a posterior vitreous detachment, and borderline for glaucoma.

It doesn't look pretty, and it's getting harder to see the pretty. Sigh...

Many of you are also going through difficulties. Problems, issues, and life changes hit hard and leave us reeling. Please remember nothing catches God by surprise, nothing is unknown, and no problem or difficulty is too big for Him to handle. Since God knows what will happen, He equips us before we are born to go through whatever we will go through.

Trouble and heartache are obstacles I would rather go around, but God says He will be there as we go **through** them. "When you pass through the waters, I will be with you; and when you pass through the rivers, they will not sweep over you. When you walk through the fire, you will not be burned; the flames will not set you ablaze." ~Isaiah 43:2 (NIV)

Whatever you face today or in the future, you can be assured, God will be with you. He won't fail or forsake you. Rest in His peace; give your worries and cares to Him because He cares about you. He will save you and quiet you with His love.

God's love, His comfort, His grace, His strength, and His peace, never fail. God's strong, loving heart will be with us through it all.

"The Lord is the one who goes ahead of you; He will be with you. He will not fail you or forsake you. Do not fear or be dismayed." ~ Deuteronomy 31:8 (NASB)

"Give all your worries and cares to God, for he cares about you." ~ 1 Peter 5:7 (NLT)

"The Lord your God in your midst, The Mighty One, will save; He will rejoice over you with gladness, He will quiet you with His love, He will rejoice over you with singing." ~ Zephaniah 3:17 (NKJV)

Time is short

I wonder how much time is left?

The message of Christ's forgiveness, salvation, and mercy is too precious to not share.

God's love is too amazing to keep to ourselves. Time is too short to waste sharing the gift we have been given.

Heavenly Father, help me not waste a moment. I want to live each day knowing it could be my last – my last opportunity to live in Your love, my last opportunity to tell someone of Your love, and my last opportunity to love with Your love. Time is too short; help me not waste a moment.

Therefore, go and make disciples of all nations, baptizing them in the name of the Father and of the Son and of the Holy Spirit. I am coming soon. Be ready; keep watch because the Son of Man will come at an hour when you do not expect Him. (Matthew 28:19, Revelation 22:20, Revelation 24:44 & 42)

Unstuck

Years ago, my sweet husband and I, being adventurous and frugal, purchased an unassembled entertainment center for our family room.

We laid the items out on the carpeting, followed the instructions (an amazing feat in itself), and within the hour had completed the project.

We knelt down and positioned ourselves to stand up the unit. The thing didn't budge. Absolutely no movement.

Uh oh.

Our assembly on the carpet had resulted in the unit being stuck to the carpet. We had to take apart the entire thing to set it free.

I've had the same problem. I've been stuck to the wrong things, stuck with the wrong people, stuck in my head, stuck in sin, stuck, and wondering if I'd ever be unstuck.

Fortunately, there is no stuck too stuck for our God. Nothing is impossible for Him, and His perfect blueprint never changes.

Looking back at my life, I can see a beautiful, loving, dismantling of me to set me free. I've been torn down to be rebuilt, dismantled to be properly assembled.

God wants the best for us and continues to work to free us from anything hindering our closeness to Him. If we don't let go of our past, we'll become trapped in our past.

When God unsticks us, let's not go back to get re-stuck. Don't chase after what God has removed.

When you are feeling dismantled, your life in shatters, remember God takes broken and creates beautiful. Pursue God and all the pieces fall into place.

You are unstuck in Christ. He has set you free, so be free!

"It was for freedom that Christ set us free." ~ Galatians 5:1

"Therefore, since we are surrounded by so great a cloud of witnesses [who by faith have testified to the truth of God's absolute faithfulness], stripping off every unnecessary weight and the sin which so easily and cleverly entangles us, let us run with endurance and active persistence the race that is set before us." ~ Hebrews 12:1 (AMP)

How dare you!

I've had atheists mad at me, furious, that I would dare talk about hell. One called it "tragic" that anyone would tell people hell exists, that there's nothing loving about talking about hell.

But I must! Since I believe in the Bible and the words that Jesus shared, it would be so very tragic and unloving if I didn't dare talk about the reality of hell and warn people about hell.

And it would be tragic and unloving if I didn't dare tell them they have a choice, a wonderful choice, to go to heaven by receiving Jesus as their Savior.

Jesus made the sacrifice for our sins, when we choose to believe in Him, give our lives to Him, we are gifted with eternal life in Heaven.

We all have a choice. For those who say no, who refuse and reject God's free offer of grace, God allows their choice. If they don't want to be with Him, although it breaks His heart, they are given their choice never to be with Him.

Hell is real. It's not a party place. It's the absence of everything good. **Anything good.** It is the absence of love.

Please don't turn away, please don't think I'm narrow-minded or a simpleton for my belief in God and His Son, Jesus Christ. If I'm wrong about hell and heaven, no harm will be done. But if I'm correct, if what I believe is true, and you refuse the offer of Jesus as Savior, your choice to turn away will be a horrible choice.

Nothing is more horrible than eternity without God. Please don't ignore the offer God has given you through the mercy of His Son, Jesus Christ. Your choice has eternal consequences.

"For God so loved the world, that He gave His only begotten Son, that whoever believes in Him shall not perish, but have eternal life. For God did not send the Son into the world to judge the world, but that the world might be saved through Him." ~ John 3:16-17 (NASB)

"And anyone who believes in God's Son has eternal life. Anyone who doesn't obey the Son will never experience eternal life but remains under God's angry judgment." ~ John 3:36 (NLT)

"For this is the will of My Father, that everyone who beholds the Son and believes in Him will have eternal life, and I Myself will raise him up on the last day." ~ John 6:40 (NASB)

"For the wages of sin is death, but the free gift of God is eternal life in Christ Jesus our Lord." ~ Romans 6:23 (NASB)

Rescue

Fall arrived on the hottest day of the week. Taking advantage of the sunny day, I decided to wash our yard sneakers we had left outside and in the garage. Not sure if spiders or some other unsightly creepy-crawly-bug thing had decided to hide in the shoes, I picked them up by their laces and threw them in the washer, started the water, closed the lid, and walked away.

A few minutes later, not sure why, I felt the urge to check the washer. I returned to the laundry room and opened the lid. The washer was continuing to fill and had not started. I peered inside, and out of the suds popped a big frog.

Poor baby had evidently been in one of the shoes. I grabbed a rag, told him I would help, prayed the Lord would tell him I was going to help, and was able to wrap him up and take him outside. Safely in the grass, the frog sat and looked at me for a few minutes, then hopped under our shed to safety.

I know to some people this was not a big thing. He was only a frog. But for me, it shows the tenderness of our loving God. I didn't know something was trapped and in danger in our washer, but God knew. He knew the frog needed rescue.

Some of you are in a situation and wonder if God knows where you are, if He knows your need, if He knows you are afraid, and you wonder if God will come to your rescue.

Dear friend, not one of God's children is unnoticed. God knows, He cares, He is with you, and His strong, loving arm is never too short to save.

Hold on, friend. God's rescue is coming.

Heavenly Father, thank You that Your love is boundless and never limited by time or space. You know every need and You promise to supply all our needs. Someone is so afraid right now and in need of rescue. Thank You for Your comforting word...

Jesus reassures, "Are not five sparrows sold for two cents? Yet not one of them is forgotten before God. Indeed, the very hairs of your head are all numbered. Do not fear; you are more valuable than many sparrows." ~ Luke 12:6-7 (NASB)

"Is anyone crying for help? God is listening, ready to rescue you." ~ Psalm 34:17 (MSG)

"Truly the eye of the Lord is on those who fear him, on those who hope in his steadfast love" ~ Psalm 33:18 (NRSV)

"Do not fear, for I am with you; do not anxiously look about you, for I am your God. I will strengthen you, surely I will help you, surely I will uphold you with My righteous right hand." ~ Isaiah 41:10 (NASB)

Come away

I sat at the computer looking through the updates online. Some shared highlights of their day, photos of themselves and family members, Bible verses, fun graphics or videos. Unfortunately, also mixed in were news reports, rants and frustrations of the state of our country and our world. I felt my soul sinking, overwhelmed at the negativity, anger, and hopelessness.

Then a quiet voice within me beckoned, "*Come away.*"

I didn't move, surprised I had a choice. Troubles and distractions are so troublesome and distracting, they pull, claw at us to pay attention to the neediness of the needs. Yet even Jesus would often withdraw to a quiet place. Even in the clamor of the world around Him, He made time, took time to step away.

There is an art of stepping away, walking away, to get back in step to walk with The One who is The Way. Like the football players who sit on the bench after a big play and reach for oxygen, we need to breathe the breath of life. We need to take time to look away from the world and look up to The One who created the world.

Jesus beckons, "*Come away.*"

Overwhelmed? Is the noise, the news, the clutter and clatter of everyday life too much? Are you gasping for breath?

Come to a quiet place and rest. Rest is found for the one who rests in Jesus.

Soul-strength is in the quietness and rest of The One who made your soul. Draw near to God, and He will draw near to you. *Come away.*

Jesus said, "Come aside by yourselves to a deserted place and rest a while...." ~ Mark 6:31 (NKJV)

"Come to Me, all who are weary and heavy-laden, and I will give you rest." ~ Matthew 11:28 (NASB)

"Be still and know that I am God; I will be exalted among the nations, I will be exalted in the earth!" ~ Psalm 46:10 (NKJV)

"The Lord is my shepherd; I shall not want. He makes me lie down in green pastures; He leads me beside quiet waters. He restores my soul..." ~ Psalm 23:1-3 (NASB)

"Draw near to God and He will draw near to you..." ~ James 4:8 (NASB)

"Cast your burden on the Lord [releasing the weight of it] and He will sustain you; He will never allow the [consistently] righteous to be moved (made to slip, fall, or fail)." ~ Psalm 55:22 (AMPC)

"For thus says the Lord God, the Holy One of Israel: In returning and rest you shall be saved; in quietness and confidence shall be your strength...." ~ Isaiah 30:15 (NKJV)

Eyes wide-open

The prompting came to study a painting I've had for almost thirty years. I looked and looked, but didn't see anything new. But then, at the base of the mountains, I observed a river. Honestly, I can't remember paying attention to that detail. But now, I see a strip of light blue that seems iridescent.

Now I see with eyes wide-open. I see what had been unnoticed. And oh, I realize in God's economy, in God's amazing reality, it's about seeing the unseen through the eyes of The One who sees all. It's about looking beyond the possible to see the impossible. It's about opening our eyes wider to the see the grandness of our Great God.

I want to see beyond earthly vision, but I have to be open to look, watch, study, and acknowledge what the Lord has done and is doing. All around us, every day, every moment, God is working.

God's handprints are all over creation. He paints His love in the sunrise and the sunsets, in the gentle breeze, and in the flowers of the field. Every heartbeat signals God's continued purpose for our lives.

Let's look beyond the ordinary. Let's see the unseen with eyes wide-open to what is beyond earthly vision.

Open my eyes, Lord. Open my eyes to notice how You are working. Open my eyes wide-open to view life from Your perspective. 'Oh, how I want to see beyond what I expect to see.

I want to see beyond the everyday usual to find the amazing unseen. Open my eyes to see the unseen!

"So, we fix our eyes not on what is seen, but on what is unseen, since what is seen is temporary, but what is unseen is eternal." ~ 2 Corinthians 4:18 (NIV)

"Now to Him who is able to do far more abundantly beyond all that we ask or think, according to the power that works within us, to Him be the glory in the church and in Christ Jesus to all generations forever and ever. Amen." ~ Ephesians 3:20-21 (NASB)

Taken away

A friend of mine grew up in a country hostile to Christians. Her mother knew the time was short to keep their Bibles, so she had her children memorize scripture. As a result, my friend could quote much of the Bible.

If tomorrow your church was taken away, your Bibles removed from your home, and you were told never to talk about Christ. What would you do?

Have you memorized scripture? Could you tell others about Christ without your pastor or Bible teacher?

Christians around the world are faced with persecution. Our time may also come when our Bibles, books, churches, teachers and pastors, and Christian artifacts are taken away. We need to be prepared. We don't need to fear, we don't need to worry, but we do need to make sure our faith is solid, sure, and grounded.

Hide God's word in your heart. Know God's truth so that you will always be able to stand firm on God's truth.

"You shall teach them diligently to your sons and shall talk of them when you sit in your house and when you walk by the way and when you lie down and when you rise up. You shall bind them as a sign on your hand and they shall be as frontals on your forehead. You shall write them on the doorposts of your house and on your gates." ~ Deuteronomy 6:6-9 (NASB)

"All Scripture is inspired by God and profitable for teaching, for reproof, for correction, for training in righteousness; so that the man of God may be adequate, equipped for every good work." ~ 2 Timothy 3:16-17 (NASB)

Shine

Hundreds of pebbles, maybe a thousand, but one caught my attention. The tiny rock had a shine that made it stand out among the rest. Assuming the stone was a crystal, I picked it up. However, upon closer inspection, I found nothing special; only a basic dull rock. The only reason the pebble had been shining was because of the sun's rays hitting the stone.

I want to shine for Jesus. Unfortunately, many days I try so hard that I make myself crazy. Thankfully, a little dull pebble finally got through my little dull skull. To shine for Jesus, I need to be with Jesus and allow His light to shine through. The world doesn't need a shiny Lisa Buffaloe, but it sure does need The Light of The World — Jesus.

Even though the moon is a big round dull rock in the sky, it beautifully reflects the light of the sun. Which gives me great hope, I might be a basic, dull rock here on earth, but I can reflect the never-ending, amazing, wonderful SONshine. So, I'm going to spend time with the Light of the World and let Him shine through.

Let's spend time with Jesus and let His light shine!

"Arise, shine; for your light has come, and the glory of the Lord has risen upon you." ~ Isaiah 60:1 (NASB) Jesus said, "I am the Light of the world; he who follows Me will not walk in the darkness but will have the Light of life." ~ John 8:12 (NASB)

"Let your light shine before men in such a way that they may see your good works and glorify your Father who is in heaven." ~ Matthew 5:16 (NASB)

"For God, who said, 'Light shall shine out of darkness,' is the One who has shone in our hearts to give the Light of the knowledge of the glory of God in the face of Christ." ~ 2 Corinthians 4:6 (NASB)

Renew the view

Stop the world, I want to get off! Anyone else feel that way? Goodness, it's crazy out there. People are worried, fearful, and angry, and with the mess of the world it's easy to get caught up in the messiness.

I need to remember to renew the view by viewing from the proper perspective of God's truth. Jesus prayed, "Sanctify them in the truth [set them apart for Your purposes, make them holy]; Your word is truth." ~ John 17:17 (AMP)

We are to be sanctified in God's truth -- set apart, dedicated, holy. As Christians, we are not of this world, our citizenship is in heaven and in that truth, we are overcomers, united and grounded in the solid rock of God's love.

We don't have to fear, because God's perfect love casts out fear. Although we are subject to government, we need to remember on Whose shoulders rests the government.

Let's pray for those in authority, living lives that show the love of God. Some trust in chariots and horses (political parties), but we can completely trust in the Lord.

Take a deep breath, cease striving and remember God is in control and over all nations. No need to be anxious or worried, God knows what you need and He's got all you need.

Trust in the Lord, He'll direct your paths.

Trust in God, rely on Him, do good, dwell in the land and be faithful. Love one another. Don't fear God is with you. Don't be afraid. Don't fear men.

Rejoice in the Lord. Rest in the Lord. Trust in the Lord. You are safe forever in God's loving hands.

(Romans 12:2, Philippians 3:20, 1 John 5:4, 1 John 4:18, 1 Timothy 2:1-2, 1 Peter 2:13, Romans 13:1-7, Isaiah 9:6, Psalm 20:7, Psalm 46:10, Philippians 4:6, Matthew 6:25-34, Proverbs 3:5-6, Psalm 37:3, John 13:34-35, Isaiah 41:10, Proverbs 29:25, Philippians 4:4, Psalm 91:1, John 10:28-29)

Sidetracked

I've been sidetracked by pain, life, the world, by opinions of others, by the news, by too many things that are not eternal. I must seek first the kingdom of God. I have to kindle afresh and fan into flame the word implanted within me.

I'm off track and need soul-food! I need to get back on track by feeding the word within me by feeding on The Word.

God's word is a lamp for my feet and a light for my path. His word is a rock, a fire, a world-changer. His word is sharper than any two-edged sword dividing bones and marrow, setting hearts afire.

Health may not be very healthy, life may not be very life-giving, the world may be so very worldly, but I'm running to The Word which is The Way to get back on track!

Heavenly Father, please forgive me for being off-track. Thank You that You are the Way. Thank You for Your Word. Help me to get my focus back on You and study Your word. Thank You that You are the life, the way, and the truth.

"Trust God from the bottom of your heart; don't try to figure out everything on your own. Listen for God's voice in everything you do, everywhere you go; he's the one who will keep you on track." ~ Proverbs 3:5-6 (MSG)

Sometimes love...

"**N**ow Jesus loved Martha and her sister and Lazarus. So, when He heard that he was sick, He then stayed two days longer in the place where He was."*

Jesus could have healed Lazarus, yet when Jesus arrived four days late, Lazarus was dead. Sometimes God's love doesn't behave in the way we wish and doesn't seem to make sense. Sometimes His love waits beyond what we think is acceptable and doesn't even seem very loving.

When Jesus finally arrived, Martha came to him and said, "Lord, if You had been here, my brother would not have died."

Jesus didn't rebuke Martha for her grief or her questions. He gently reminded Martha, "Did I not tell you that if you believe, you will see the glory of God?" Then Jesus called Lazarus out from the grave.

Sometimes God's love doesn't come on our timing, so a greater love can come on God's timing. Lazarus wasn't just healed from disease; he was healed from death.

No pain, no heartache, no suffering, not even death can keep our Savior from saving. The love of Jesus resurrects, restores, redeems, and brings life from death.

Because of hardship, pain, grief, or difficult situation, do you wonder if God loves you?

Oh friend, you may question God's love, but your questions never limit the love of God.

God's love is never bound by space or time, for there is nothing impossible for our loving God.

Even when you don't understand, even when God seems far away, God's love never fails, and His love will never fail you.

Heavenly Father, sometimes Your love seems so far away. Sometimes Your love seems to wait too long. Often I don't understand what is happening in my life and in the world, but even though I can't see You, I will trust You will come, and You will resurrect, restore, redeem, and bring new life. Thank You that nothing is impossible for Your unfailing love. Help me to trust and wait on You.

John 11:5-6 (NASB), John 11:21 (NASB), John 11:40 (NIV)

Breathless expectation

"To be certain of God means that we are uncertain in all our ways, not knowing what tomorrow may bring. This is generally expressed with a sigh of sadness, but it should be an expression of breathless expectation. We are uncertain of the next step, but we are certain of God As soon as we abandon ourselves to God and do the task He has placed closest to us, He begins to fill our lives with surprises." ~ Oswald Chambers, *My Utmost for His Highest*

Breathless expectation.

Oh my. Can you imagine awakening every morning in breathless expectation of our amazing God? I want to live like that!

The disciples who walked with Jesus, each day saw something new, something amazing. They watched as Jesus healed, cast out demons, walked on water, and calmed stormy seas. Each day held breathless expectation of incredible wonders.

I have wonderful news, those of us who have Jesus living within us, have the power of God within us, therefore we can walk with our Savior in breathless expectation. Every day is a new day with our amazing God. Let's live in breathless expectation!

Lord, I want to live in breathless expectation of You. Open my eyes to watch You work, open my mind to be fully aware of You. May my every breath catch in breathless expectation of Your wonders.

Don't skim through the best

We are blessed to live in an age with an amazing array of books, Bible studies, online studies and devotionals to assist us in our faith-walk. I am so grateful God has placed teachers in the body of Christ. Pastors, Bible teachers, scholars, and writers can give clarity and truth to help us in our growth as Christians.

Iron sharpens iron, and how grateful I am for those who sharpen me deeper into God and His Word. I love reading an author who sees something in scripture and with the Holy Spirit's guidance can point us to see things with fresh eyes.

Unfortunately, when reading, I'm embarrassed I've often caught myself skimming through familiar verses to read what the author has written. However, I don't need to stop reading other authors or listening to pastors or Bible teachers, I just need to be careful not to skim over the best. God's word, His words are the only words that truly bring life, they are the BEST words.

Goodness, I want to remember to pay the utmost attention to scripture. Then, I can enjoy the blessings of mining God's truth with my brothers and sisters in Christ.

God's word is a treasure chest filled with heavenly wisdom jewels, and there is nothing more exciting than discovering God's best.

Let's continue listening, reading, and growing but never skim over God's best.

Heavenly Father, help Your word **pop** and highlight on every page I read and pop in my mind on every sermon and Bible study talk I hear. I want Your word to be the most important words in my life. I love You, Father!

"When I discovered your words, I devoured them. They are my joy and my heart's delight, for I bear your name, O Lord God of Heaven's Armies." ~ Jeremiah 15:16 (NLT)

"The sum of Your word is truth, and every one of Your righteous ordinances is everlasting." ~ Psalm 119:160 (NASB)

"Your word I have treasured in my heart, that I may not sin against You." ~ Psalm 119:11 (NASB)

"How sweet are Your words to my taste, sweeter than honey to my mouth!" ~ Psalm 119:103 (NKJV)

I'm telling

Tell others about God.

Tell them how God saved you.
Tell them what God has done for you.
Tell what God has done for others.
Tell your children, friends, family, those you know, and those you meet, about God.
Tell of God's amazing love.
Tell of God's wonderful grace.
Tell of God's bountiful mercy.
Even "the heavens are telling of the glory of God; and their expanse is declaring the work of His hands" (Psalm 19:1 NASB).

Will you tell?

"I will give thanks to the LORD with all my heart; I will tell of all Your wonders. Come and hear, all who fear God, and I will tell of what He has done for my soul. My mouth shall tell of Your righteousness and of Your salvation all day long; For I do not know the sum of them. But as for me, the nearness of God is my good; I have made the Lord GOD my refuge, That I may tell of all Your works. Tell to the generations to come the praises of the LORD, and His strength and His wondrous works that He has done. That the generation to come might know, even the children yet to be born, that they may arise and tell them to their children.

So, we Your people and the sheep of Your pasture will give thanks to You forever; to all generations we will tell of Your praise. Tell of His glory among the nations, His wonderful deeds among all the peoples. Men shall speak of the power of Your awesome acts, And I will tell of Your greatness. But we [ourselves] cannot help telling what we have seen and heard."

Let's tell everyone about our wonderful Savior and God!

(Psalm 9:1, Psalm 66:16, 71:15, 73:28, 78:4, 78:6, 79:13, 96:3, 145:6 NASB, Acts 4:20AMP)

Don't Lose

You lose with sin. Sin is loss. Sin results in negative consequences. Sin blocks God, destroys, and kills. You lose relationship with God. You lose blessings. You lose being used for God's glory. You lose part of you. You lose.

Salvation (forgiveness for sins) comes through Jesus Christ. For if you accept Jesus as Savior, and ask Him into your heart, you lose your sins, they are gone and you are given a new life.

You can choose your own way. You can go off on your own paths, or you can choose God and His Son, Jesus Christ. Please don't turn away, because turning away from Jesus leads to eternal loss. Please don't lose.

Don't be a loser. Be a winner by choosing Jesus!

"God loved the world so much that he gave his one and only Son so that whoever believes in him may not be lost, but have eternal life. God did not send his Son into the world to judge the world guilty, but to save the world through him. People who believe in God's Son are not judged guilty. Those who do not believe have already been judged guilty, because they have not believed in God's one and only Son. Jesus answered, 'I am the way, and the truth, and the life. The only way to the Father is through me'" (John 3:16-18, John 14:6 NCV).

Called to speak

Jesus said, "What I tell you in the darkness, speak in the light; and what you hear whispered in your ear, proclaim upon the housetops." ~ Matthew 10:27 (NASB).

We are called to be speakers. We can speak God's truth. We can speak The Truth in love.

Speak The Truth.
Speak in Love.
Speak

"Which things we also **speak**, not in words taught by human wisdom, but in those taught by the Spirit, combining spiritual thoughts with spiritual words. Having the same spirit of faith, according to what is written, 'I believed; therefore, I spoke,' **we also believe; therefore, we also speak**.

Speaking the truth in love, we are to grow up in all aspects into Him who is the head, even Christ. **Speaking to one another in psalms and hymns and spiritual songs**, singing and making melody with your heart to the Lord.

Laying aside falsehood, **speak truth** each one of you with his neighbor, for we are members of one another. Just as we have been approved by God to be entrusted with the gospel, so **we speak, not as pleasing men, but God** who examines our hearts.

Speak the things which are fitting for sound doctrine. Whoever speaks, is to do so as one who is speaking the utterances of God; whoever serves is to do so as one who is serving by the strength which God supplies; so that in all things God may be glorified through Jesus Christ, to whom belongs the glory and dominion forever and ever. Amen."*

Speak The Truth in love.
Speak The Truth.
Speak in Love.
Speak the utterances of God.

(1 Corinthians 2:13, 2 Corinthians 4:13, Ephesians 4:15, Ephesians 5:19, Ephesians 4:25, 1 Thessalonians 2:4, Titus 2:1, 1 Peter 4:11 NASB).

Cardboard testimonies

A video from a church showed people using a piece of cardboard to write what they were before God, and then flip it over to reveal who they are now in Christ.

I too have my own testimony, my cardboard filled with heartache and pain, yet restored and redeemed by an amazing God.

The more trials I have endured, the more I see God's unending faithfulness and love. With each hurdle crossed, each skirmish survived, comes strength, fulfillment, and joy. I knew God loved me, but I did not understand the depth and width of His love until I walked through the long valleys.

Nothing has been enjoyable about suffering and pain, but I wouldn't change it for the world, because through it all I have grown closer to the God who created, formed, and loved me before I was born. God's word tells us, "When you pass through the waters, I will be with you; and when you pass through the rivers, they will not sweep over you. When you walk through the fire, you will not be burned; the flames will not set you ablaze" (Isaiah 43:2 NIV).

God never fails. No sin is too dark for God's grace-filled touch. No trauma is too traumatic for God's healing love.

Nothing is impossible with God. He is a God of restoration and redemption.

Whatever your pain, no matter how dark your past, God's love never fails.

Whatever you were, whatever happened to you, allow God to flip the past with His unfailing love, healing, grace, and restoration.

Respect and fear

I've been wondering, why doesn't the world respect, fear, and love God?

Does the world not respond, love, and respect God, because God's children aren't showing them the way?

Oh dear, I want to remember, and I want to show the world that...

The fear of the Lord is pure enduring forever ~ Psalm 19:9.

The fear of the Lord is the beginning of wisdom; all who follow his precepts have good understanding. ~ Psalm 111:10.

The fear of the Lord adds length to life ~ Proverbs 10:27.

The fear of the Lord is a fountain of life ~ Proverbs 14:27.

The fear of the Lord teaches a man wisdom, and humility ~ Proverbs 15:33.

Through love and faithfulness sin is atoned for; through the fear of the Lord a man avoids evil ~ Proverbs 16:6.

The fear of the Lord leads to life: Then one rests content, untouched by trouble ~Proverbs 19:23.

Humility and the fear of the Lord bring wealth and honor and life ~ Proverbs 22:4.

Let's show the world the wondrous beauty and blessings of the fear of the Lord!

Dwelling and abiding

Can you imagine dwelling with God, staying in the shadow of His wings; remaining with Him forever, held continually safe, abiding in His love. Oh my, what joy! Yes, please. May I? Please, please, please?

As I was digging in God's word, I found these wonderful truths using the original Hebrew definitions.

I love the intimacy of God's word, the absolute wrapping of His arms around our hearts. As you read the truths, what words stand out to you?

He who **dwells** (*remain, sit, abide, have one's abode, to stay*) in the **shelter** (*covering, shelter, hiding place, secret place*) of the Most High will **abide** (*lodge, remain, dwell*) in the shadow of the Almighty.

Jesus said, **Dwell** (*to remain, abide, to sojourn, tarry, not to depart, to continue to be present, to be held, kept, continually, to continue to be, not to perish, to last, endure, live, in, to remain as one)* in Me, and I will **dwell** in you.

Just as no branch can bear fruit of itself without abiding in the vine, neither can you bear fruit unless you **abide** in Me.

If you keep my commandments, you will **abide** *to remain, sojourn, tarry, not to depart, to continue to be present, to be held, kept, continually, to continue to be, not to perish, to last, endure, to remain as one)* in my love, just as I have kept my Father's commandments and **abide** in his love.*

Heavenly Father, thank You that we can dwell, remain, sit, abide, have our abode, stay, lodge, sojourn, tarry, never to depart, continue to be present, held, kept continually, continue to not perish, to last, endure, live, and remain as one with You.

*(Emphasis added on scripture, Psalm 91:1, John 15:4, John 15:10)

Morning prayer

Would you be willing to join me in a morning prayer?

Good morning, Lord. I adore You. I worship You. You are my love; You are the One who knows me inside and out and continues to love. Thank You. Thank You for Your unfailing love. Thank You for another day. Help me to serve You well, to love You with all my heart, soul, mind, and strength. Oh, to be lost in Your Love, Lord! Lost in You so completely I fade away and Your love flows free.

Open my eyes to see the beauty of You. Take me away so I may be found in You. Let Your living water flow in and through me. Let Your Bread of Heaven nourish my soul so that I may nourish the souls of others.

May The Word, The Truth, and The Life, bless me with His words, truth, and life to share with a dying world so desperate for words of truth and life.

Oh, to be lost in Your love, Lord. So completely lost in You, that all I do and say may bring You glory and honor.

Help me to always tell others of Your beautiful, amazing, grace, mercy, and love. Oh Father, open closed hearts to Your wonderful love. Open blind eyes to see You! Fall fresh, Lord. Fall fresh on us so that our lives will touch other lives for You. Thank You, Lord. Praise You, Lord! I love You, Father!

"...as for me, I shall sing of Your strength; yes, I shall joyfully sing of Your lovingkindness in the morning ...." ~ Psalm 59:16 (NASB)

Extravagant, never failing

"God has never failed me. Even in my greatest difficulties, heaviest trials, and deepest poverty and need. He has never failed me. Because I was enabled by God's grace to trust Him. He has always come to my aid. I delight in speaking well of His name." ~ George Mueller

I can say the same, God has never failed me. Even on days when I wonder where He is and why my situation doesn't change, God has never failed me. Even when I couldn't see what would happen next, (even when I didn't like what would happen next) God has never failed me.

Even when I wallowed in the mud of sin or self-pity, God picked me up, dusted me off, and set me on my feet again, granting unfailing, unmerited, grace and favor. He has never failed to bless me with food when the pantry was bare. He has never failed to hold me close in times of sorrow.

God has never failed to heal the wounds of the past. He has never failed to grant beauty through His wonderful creation. He has never failed to supply my every need. Everyday God never fails to lavish His extravagant love.

Sweet Heavenly Father, I delight in speaking well of Your name. Open my eyes to always see how You have worked in my life and how You are working. Capture my heart again in Your extravagant, intimate, intoxicating, unfailing love.

"How priceless is your unfailing love, O God! People take refuge in the shadow of your wings." ~ Psalm 36:7 (NIV)

"The amazing grace of the Master, Jesus Christ, the extravagant love of God, the intimate friendship of the Holy Spirit, be with all of you." ~ 2 Corinthians 13:14 (MSG)

The Thing

I don't know about you, but there are times the things in this world call and beckon and cling and claw, dragging me down or veering me off-course of God's perfect path.

So, I've decided unless the Lord brings the thing, orchestrates the thing, does the thing, and wants me to have the thing, I don't want the thing!

Heavenly Father, help me to not want any "thing" that You don't want me to have. I want Your best and Your perfect will. Help me to set my mind on the things above, not on the things on the earth. Thank You that every perfect gift comes from You, help me to look to You for any "thing", anything, every "thing", and every thing!

"Set your mind on the things above, not on the things that are on earth." ~ Colossians 3:2 (NASB)

"The young lions do lack and suffer hunger; but they who seek the Lord shall not be in want of any good thing." ~ Psalm 34:10 (NASB)

"I will cry to God Most High, to God who accomplishes all things for me." ~ Psalm 57:2 (NASB)

"For the Lord God is a sun and shield; The Lord gives grace and glory; no good thing does He withhold from those who walk uprightly." ~ Psalm 84:11 (NASB)

Don't forget

Don't Forget ...

Regardless of how other people treat you, see you, or don't see you.

Regardless of how you feel.

Regardless of your circumstances.

Regardless of where you've been, what you've done, or what has been done to you.

Don't Ever Forget THE Truth.

God always sees you, loves you, will never fail you, will never forsake you, can always forgive you, always restore you, and always redeems.

God loves you!

Guilt

I realized something this morning, something I need to remember. We don't need to feel guilty for not doing what we are **not** called to do.

If God has called us to do something, then we need to do it. (If we run from His calling watch out for whales — just ask Jonah.)

We don't need to listen to Satan's lies that we need to do everything and feel guilty if we aren't doing everything.

If we are following God, He'll show us the way.

So, let's be still, relax and rest.

Take a deep breath, and when guilt comes calling, call on God. God loves us. He's always in control. When frustrated about everything, take everything to God.

Be still. Relax. Rest. God is in control.

"He has shown you, O mortal, what is good. And what does the Lord require of you? To act justly and to love mercy and to walk humbly with your God." ~ Micah 6:8 (NIV)

"Jesus replied: 'Love the Lord your God with all your heart and with all your soul and with all your mind.' This is the first and greatest commandment." ~ Matthew 22:37-38 (NIV)

"Cease striving and know that I am God; I will be exalted among the nations, I will be exalted in the earth." ~ Psalm 46:10 (NASB)

Worried?

A loved one came to mind, and I started to worry.

Then truth came ...Is there any situation that you (or your loved one) will encounter that is too difficult for God? Is there anything too hard for God?

The answer of course is No!

Nothing is impossible for God. There is nothing we will encounter that is too difficult for God.

God's loving arms are never too short to save. There is nowhere I can go (or my loved ones can go) outside of God's reach.

As I pondered God's truth, peace came. God's truth sets us free and brings peace.

Are you worried? Run to God's truth.

Cease striving, be still, remember and know that He is God, nothing is impossible for Him, rest in His peace.

"Cease striving and know that I am God; I will be exalted among the nations; I will be exalted in the earth." ~ Psalm 46:10 (NASB)

"For nothing will be impossible with God." ~ Luke 1:37 (NASB)

"Peace I leave with you; My peace I give to you; not as the world gives do I give to you. Do not let your heart be troubled, nor let it be fearful." ~ John 14:27 (NASB)

He leads

"Your ears will hear a word behind you, 'This is the way, walk in it,' whenever you turn to the right or to the left." ~ Isaiah 30:21 (NASB)

I love that verse! I've loved the verse for years, quoted it, meditated on it, and was so grateful for it. But to be honest I still worried I might turn the wrong way, not a sinful way just the wrong way.

Maybe God would want me to go left and I would go right. Like a little lost kid, I'd be cluelessly wandering off on some God-forsaken pathway all alone without God's guidance.

All alone. All by myself. Lost. Alone. Whimper. Sniffle. Waaaaaaaail!

Thankfully God doesn't leave; He is a God who continues to reach out, to call, to beckon. If I'm turning left, He will guide. If I'm turning right, He'll guide me. He will tell me the right way or the wrong way no matter which way I go. I'm so grateful. No matter how clueless I may be, God will guide. I tell ya, that is a reason to celebrate!

Our God will lead us. His word promises...

"'I will feed My flock and I will lead them to rest,' declares the Lord God." ~ Ezekiel 34:15 (NASB)

"Like a shepherd He will tend His flock, In His arm He will gather the lambs and carry them in His bosom; He will gently lead the nursing ewes." ~ Isaiah 40:11

"I will lead the blind by a way they do not know, in paths they do not know I will guide them. I will make darkness into light before them and rugged places into plains. These are the things I will do, and I will not leave them undone." ~ Isaiah 42:16

"They will not hunger or thirst, nor will the scorching heat or sun strike them down; for He who has compassion on them will lead them and will guide them to springs of water." ~ Isaiah 49:10

"Thanks be to God, who always leads us in triumph in Christ, and manifests through us the sweet aroma of the knowledge of Him in every place." ~ 2 Corinthians 2:14

Feeling lost? All alone? Wondering if you went the wrong way? Praise the Lord, our God will lead us!

Make me Yours

This ache, this longing inside can only be filled by You. Heavenly Father, quiet my soul with Your love.

Fill my heart with Your joy.

Make me Yours. Completely Yours.

Infuse me with Your presence. Remove me so that You may be all in me.

May You, the Great I AM, be all there is in me.

May I yield to Your will.

May I bend to Your ways.

May I walk in Your path.

May I breathe with Your breath.

May I love with Your love.

May I be all Yours now and forever.

I desire to desire Your desire. Stretch my soul to look beyond the natural. I desire to joy in what brings You joy. I want to see through Your eyes and hear with Your ears. I long to walk on Your perfect path. Make my heart beat in time with Yours.

"Your unfailing love is better than life itself; how I praise you! I've kept my feet on the ground, I've cultivated a quiet heart. Like a baby content in its mother's arms, my soul is a baby content." ~ Psalm 63:3 (NLT), Psalm 131:2 (MSG)

What is your prayer to the Lord?

Personal Help

There are days the journey is difficult, and the trials are many. If you are going through hardships, I've placed these verses to give you hope. God's word is for you.

The Bible contains a rich storehouse of treasure verses to help us through whatever difficulties we may face.

When we take time to not only read God's word but remember His words are written personally for us, we can find the peace and joy of His presence.

Would you be willing to read and make them personal?

I can do everything through Him who gives me strength, for all things are possible with God. The Lord is my strength and my song; He has become my salvation. When anxiety was great within me, His consolation brought joy to my soul. The Lord is my strength and my shield; my heart trusts in Him, and I am helped. My heart leaps for joy and I will give thanks to Him in song.

I will consider it pure joy, when I face trials of many kinds, because the Sovereign Lord is my strength; He makes my feet like the feet of a deer, He enables me to go on the heights. He will cover me with His feathers, and under His wings I find refuge; His faithfulness will be my shield and rampart. For, those who sow in tears will reap with songs of joy.

The LORD is my strength and my shield; my heart trusts in him, and I am helped. My heart leaps for joy and I will give thanks to him in song.

Let all who take refuge in You be glad; let them ever sing for joy. Spread Your protection over them, that those who love Your name may rejoice in You.

To Him who is able to keep me from falling and to present me before His glorious presence without fault and with great joy— to the only God our Savior be glory, majesty, power and authority, through Jesus Christ our Lord, before all ages, now and forevermore! Amen.

(Philippians 4:13, Mark 10:27, Psalm 118:14, Psalm 94:19, Psalm 28:7, James 1:2, Habakkuk 3:19, Psalm 91:4, Psalm 126:5, Psalm 28:7, Psalm 5:11, and Jude 1:24-25)

Lifeblood

The other day I was pondering our amazing bodies. Blood travels throughout the body, then returns to the heart and lungs to receive oxygen which regenerates, renews, restores, and refreshes. Is that not truly amazing?

In the same way, when we are told to love the Lord with all our hearts, the lifeblood of our heart is regenerated, renewed, restored, and refreshed through the loving heart of the Breath of Life. Now that is amazing – our God is AMAZING!

Heavenly Father, thank You for Your lifeblood that pours into our physical and spiritual hearts. Help me to keep my heart beating in complete love for You.

"You shall love the Lord your God with all your heart, and with all your soul, and with all your mind." ~ Matthew 22:37 (NASB)

"...the love of God has been poured out within our hearts through the Holy Spirit who was given to us." ~ Romans 5:5 (NASB)

"Therefore, we do not lose heart, but though our outer man is decaying, yet our inner man is being renewed day by day." ~ 2 Corinthians 4:16 (NASB)

Psalming into the new

I'm having the most fun thinking about the Psalms and how God gave us visuals in the New Testament through His Son, Jesus. I think I could spend several months discovering the beautiful images of His love and provision.

Here are just a few examples of what I found....

"Let all who seek You rejoice and be glad in You; let those who love Your salvation say continually, 'The Lord be magnified!'" ~ Psalm 40:16 (NASB)

"Zacchaeus was trying to see who Jesus was, and was unable because of the crowd, for he was small in stature. So, he ran on ahead and climbed up into a sycamore tree in order to see Him, for He was about to pass through that way. When Jesus came to the place, He looked up and said to him, 'Zacchaeus, hurry and come down, for today I must stay at your house.' And he hurried and came down and received Him gladly. ...And Jesus said to him, 'Today salvation has come to this house, ...for the Son of Man has come to seek and to save that which was lost." ~ Luke 19:3-10 (NASB)

"He calms the storm, so that its waves are still." ~ Psalm 107:29 (NKJV)

"Jesus stood up and commanded the wind and said to the waves, 'Quiet! Be still!' Then the wind stopped, and it became completely calm." ~ Mark 4:39 (NCV)

"Bless the Lord, O my soul, and forget none of His benefits, Who pardons all your iniquities, Who heals all your diseases." ~ Psalm 103:2-3 (NASB)

"The news about Jesus spread all over Syria, and people brought all the sick to him. They were suffering from different kinds of diseases. Some were in great pain, some had demons, some were epileptics, and some were paralyzed. Jesus healed all of them." ~ Matthew 4:24 (NCV)

"The Lord is my shepherd; I shall not want." ~ Psalm 23:1 (NKJV)

"I am the good shepherd. The good shepherd gives His life for the sheep." ~ John 10:11 (NKJV)

"For He looked down from His holy height; from heaven the Lord gazed upon the earth, to hear the groaning of the prisoner, to set free those who were doomed to death." ~ Psalm 102:19-20 (NASB)

Jesus said, "The Spirit of the Lord is on me, because he has anointed me to proclaim good news to the poor. He has sent me to proclaim freedom for the prisoners and recovery of sight for the blind, to set the oppressed free, to proclaim the year of the Lord's favor." ~ Luke 4:18-19 (NIV)

"He gives justice to the oppressed and food to the hungry. The Lord frees the prisoners." ~ Psalm 146:7 (NLT)

"...Jesus took the five loaves and two fish, looked up toward heaven, and blessed them. Then, breaking the loaves into pieces, he gave the bread to the disciples, who distributed it to the people. They all ate as much as they wanted, and afterward, the disciples picked up twelve baskets of leftovers. About 5,000 men were fed that day, in addition to all the women and children!" ~ Matthew 14:19-21 (NLT) "...if the Son makes you free, you shall be free indeed." ~ John 8:36 (NKJV)

"He sent from above, he took me, he drew me out of many waters." ~ Psalm 18:16 (KJV)

Peter said to Him, "Lord, if it is You, command me to come to You on the water." And He said, "Come!" And Peter got out of the boat, and walked on the water and came toward Jesus. But seeing the wind, he became frightened, and beginning to sink, he cried out, "Lord, save me!" Immediately Jesus stretched out His hand and took hold of him, and said to him, "You of little faith, why did you doubt?" When they got into the boat, the wind stopped. ~ Matthew 14:28-32 (NASB)

"He will fulfill the desire of those who fear Him; He will also hear their cry and will save them." ~ Psalm 145:19 (NASB)

"For God so loved the world, that He gave His only begotten Son, that whoever believes in Him shall not perish, but have eternal life. For God did not send the Son into the world to judge the world, but that the world might be saved through Him." ~ John 3:16-17 (NASB) "For the Son of Man has come to seek and to save that which was lost." ~ Luke 19:10 (NASB)

I love discovering the beauty of God's word and the beauty of The Word. Jesus reveals the facets of God's love to us through scripture and the loving fulfillment of scripture.

Would you be willing to take time over the next few days to dig into the Psalms and look for corresponding visuals given through Jesus? I guarantee a fun adventure and very worth your time. Have fun discovering!

Heavenly Father, thank You for Your Word. Thank You for the rich, unending, amazing, wonderful discoveries we can make when we enjoy and study what You have revealed throughout the ages.

"Let the word of Christ dwell in you richly in all wisdom...." ~ Colossians 3:16 (NKJV)

The Ultimate Valentine

The holiday scheduled for Valentine's Day can be met with joy or sorrow. I have good news, every day of the week, God is crazy about you. He loves you with a pure, sweet, gentle, compassionate, merciful, unfailing love. He loves YOU!

He loves you non-stop with a non-stopping love. For the lover of your soul, how will you respond? Will you give God more of your time? More of your life? More of your heart? More of you?

Tell God of your love. Thank Him for the beauty of the sunrise and sunsets. Thank Him for rain that makes crops grow, and snow that muffles and blankets the world in white. Thank Him for laughter, for the wag of a puppy, the purr of a kitten.

Thank Him for the breath you breathe. Thank Him that He died that you may live. He gave His all, so you could have His all. God gave the ultimate valentine — His Son — for you. And you, His valentine, are greatly loved and dearly prized.

"For God so greatly loved and dearly prized the world that He [even] gave up His only begotten (unique) Son, so that whoever believes in (trusts in, clings to, relies on) Him shall not perish (come to destruction, be lost) but have eternal (everlasting) life. For God did not send the Son into the world in order to judge (to reject, to condemn, to pass sentence on) the world, but that the world might find salvation and be made safe and sound through Him." ~ John 3:16-17 (AMP)

Stuck and Trapped

Throughout Biblical history people (and nations) found themselves stuck and trapped in sticky situations.

Peter was stuck in prison, yet through the power of prayer he was released (Acts 12:1-19).

Paul and Silas were imprisoned. As they praised God their chains fell off and the prison doors were opened. The men were in prison but the jailer was the one imprisoned, and through the testimony of Paul and Silas the jailer and his family were saved (Acts 16:22-40).

Daniel was thrown in a lion's den, but God kept him safe and thus proved the greatness of God, the One True God (Daniel 6).

John stuck on Patmos received and wrote the book of Revelation.

Joseph was sold in slavery and then in prison, yet God used that time to form a young man for the saving of many lives (story starts in Genesis 37).

Moses thought he was stuck in the desert tending sheep; however, God used that time to form him into the man who would lead the Israelites to freedom (story starts in Exodus).

The Israelites were stuck at the Red Sea, but God parted the waters and led them across on dry land (Exodus 14).

Through each situation, God's glory shines and our vision is enlarged on the power of prayer, the power of praise, and the greatness and sufficiency of our God.

Stuck and feeling trapped?

Stuck is a stepping point to display the greatness of God.

Stuck is the place for faith to grow.

Stuck is the impossible place where the impossible becomes possible.

"For nothing will be impossible with God." Luke 1:37 (NASB)

Whose you are

The Israelites didn't enter the promised land and wandered for forty years in the desert because they forgot Whose they were. Taking the land wasn't about their power or size, it was about trusting the power and size of the Almighty God.

If they had remembered all the Lord had done, all the power of God's deliverance and provision, they wouldn't have hesitated. Their STRONG God was on their side, and He was the one who told them to go. Therefore, that meant He would go with them to fight for them.

Oh, how I want to get this! I want to remember Whose I am, to remember my Father God loves me and is an all-powerful God.

There is nothing standing in our way when God has told us to walk in His way.

Remember Who you belong to and Whose you are!

"Be strong and courageous, do not be afraid or tremble at them, for the Lord our God is the one who goes with you. He will not fail you or forsake you." ~ Deuteronomy 31:6 (NASB)

Be strong!

Our son loved the imaginary mechanical/robotic suits worn by some of his cartoon heroes. He thought it would be so cool to step into something strong and powerful to defeat an enemy.

Scientists have actually developed robotic hands, arms, legs and now full mechanical frames to help those who have had spinal cord injuries to walk.

In a much more powerful way, we have the Spirit of Christ living within us working to walk us through whatever we are called to walk through and to defeat our enemies.

Notice this verse, "Be strong in the Lord [draw your strength from Him and be empowered through your union with Him] and in the power of His [boundless] might" ~ Ephesians 6:10 (AMP).

Be strong **IN the Lord**. Strength doesn't come from our limited bodies; **true and unlimited strength comes from God**.

Read and know His Word (the Bible), remember all God has done, remember He created everything so He can take care of anything.

You are never powerless. Regardless of how difficult your situation, you are never without God's power. In Christ, you have power to stand in the gap for your family and friends, your nation, and this world. You have power to stand in prayer.

Through Christ we have power that breaks strongholds, sets captives free, and demolishes any barrier erected by the enemy. God's power is unlimited, ALL-mighty, and ALL-powerful!

<u>Be strong IN the Lord!</u>

"Finally, **be strong in the Lord and in his mighty power**. Put on the full armor of God, so that you can take your stand against the devil's schemes. For our struggle is not against flesh and blood, but against the rulers, against the authorities, against the powers of this dark world and against the spiritual forces of evil in the heavenly realms. Therefore, put on the full armor of God, so that when the day of evil comes, you may be able to stand your ground, and after you have done everything, to stand. Stand firm then, with the belt of truth buckled around your waist, with the breastplate of righteousness in place, and with your feet fitted with the readiness that comes from the gospel of peace. In addition to all this, take up the shield of faith, with which you can extinguish all the flaming arrows of the evil one. Take the helmet of salvation and the sword of the Spirit, which is the word of God. And pray in the Spirit on all occasions with all kinds of prayers and requests. With this in mind, be alert and always keep on praying for all the Lord's people." ~ Ephesians 6:10-18 (NIV) (emphasis added).

The Glory Comes

Dark clouds gather on the horizon, heartaches come, and trying to understand only makes things less easy to understand. At times all we can process is the processing of our pain.

Mary and Martha didn't understand why Jesus didn't rush to Bethany when they sent word their brother, Lazarus was ill. The sisters didn't understand why Jesus didn't come and why their brother died (see John 11).

Jesus arrived, but in the sorrow-filled eyes of Mary and Martha, Jesus had come too late. If Jesus had come earlier, Lazarus wouldn't have died. They question and wonder why, didn't Jesus love them, didn't Jesus love their brother? Why didn't Jesus come?

But then Jesus replied, "Did I not tell you that if you believe, you will see the glory of God?" John 11:40 (NIV)

Jesus, in His glorious might, did a glorious thing and called Lazarus from the grave.

Beyond what can be seen with human eyes, beyond the pain and frustration, hope comes. Beyond the pain and tragedy, the glory of God is working.

There's glory beyond the pain and glory beyond the suffering. There's glory beyond all the heartache of this world because Jesus comes bringing eternal hope and eternal life.

We have to believe to see beyond earthly life, to stand firm on God's promises and truth.

God won't leave or forsake you. God's love is unfailing.

There is nothing that happened, nothing that will happen, nothing that might happen, that God will not be there to help you through. "For I know the plans I have for you, declares the LORD, plans to prosper you and not to harm you, plans to give you hope and a future" ~ Jeremiah 29:11 (NIV).

No matter how dark, His glory comes.

Hold on to God's glory. Hold on to His truth. Hold on, for the glory of the risen Son will rise on your circumstance. God's glory will always come.

"Arise, shine; for your light has come, and the glory of the Lord has risen upon you." ~ Isaiah 60:1 (NASB)

Fight back

I've been in a battle; a long, hard, messy, frustrating, defeating, depressing, lonely, desert dry, hard, hard, hard battle with the enemy. Through prayer and God's word, I've made headway, felt the worst was over, then the enemy would hit again, and I'd flounder in misery and try to move forward, try to keep my eyes on God.

I sensed the Lord's Spirit telling me as a Christian I have the power of Christ. Not just a little power, we are talking **THE POWER OF CHRIST.**

As I pondered this truth, I realized God's power is always available to us as Christians because Christ lives within us. His power, His Word, His victory is available to combat against Satan.

When Jesus was confronted by Satan in the wilderness, Jesus quoted scripture (see Matthew 4). I can whimper and cry all day at the enemy, but when I quote scripture as Jesus did, that is when I find God's power.

God's truth is our offensive weapon, our sword of the Spirit so that we can fight back against the enemy. (Ephesians 6:17). **What is written** is the truth and The truth sets us free.

To help me remember, I listed some of the truths of what I'm given as a believer and follower in Jesus Christ.

As a Christian, I have Christ within me. I have His power. I can do all things through Christ who strengthens me. I am never powerless with the power of Christ.

Even when I am weak, He is strong. His strength is within me. I have **HIS POWER**. And **nothing is impossible for God**!

As a Christian, I have wisdom for every problem and situation, for God gives wisdom generously without reproach to all who ask.

As a Christian, I'll know the way, because Jesus is The Way.

As a Christian, I have the love of the Father living inside me. I can love even when my love is waning. I can love the unlovely because I am loved by the loveliest even when I was the most unlovable.

As a Christian, I have hope, even when I can't see a reason to hope, God's hope is eternal and thus I can hope. He is hope so I am never hopeless.

As a Christian, I am given the joy of Jesus. Even when I don't feel joy, Jesus lives in my heart so His joy is within my heart. So, I'll get myself out of the way with all the emotions (and lack of emotions) and will allow Jesus' joy to joyfully bubble up and out of me.

As a Christian, I have God's truth. The world is so confusing sometimes, life is so confusing, but God's truth stands firm. He will guide me in His truth.

As a Christian, I am graced with eternal life. Even when my brain and body feel lifeless, His life courses through my veins to give His abundant life.

As a Christian, I have the peace from The Prince of peace. And His peace passes the world's understanding.

As a Christian, I have the blessing of God's comfort through His Holy Spirit.

As a Christian, I have God's presence. I need never be lonely. I'm never without a friend. A true friend. A loving friend. And am never without a home for my heart.

Then I went to the Lord in prayer. Since **God's truth is <u>the power</u>**, I took verses that applied to my situation. Throughout scripture there are verses that address our fears, concerns, and difficulties.

Nehemiah went to the Lord to ask for help so I used part of his prayer to begin mine...I beseech You, O Lord God of heaven, the great and awesome God, who preserves the covenant and lovingkindness for those who love Him and keep His commandments, let Your ear now be attentive and Your eyes open to hear the prayer of Your servant which I am praying before You now. O Lord, I beseech You, may Your ear be attentive to the prayer of Your servant who delights to revere Your name (Nehemiah 1:5-6, 11).

I then used verses to apply to address the areas where I was under attack.

Whatever you are facing, wherever you feel the assault of the enemy go to God's Word and use your offensive weapons. As Jesus did with Satan, you too can respond with scripture to make the enemy flee.

I've included some examples where I took verses made them personal and responded to each issue.

There are many other verses that will apply, this is only a small sampling. **We are never left defenseless against the enemy.**

If Satan is coming at you with **feelings of loneliness – It is written...** As the Father loves

Jesus, so Jesus loves me (John 15:9). The Lord God goes with me. He will not fail me or forsake me. (Deuteronomy 31:6) Jesus calls me friend (John 15:15) God promises, "My presence shall go with you, and I will give you rest." (Exodus 33:14).

If Satan is coming at you with the **feelings of being unsettled, not feeling at home – It is written...**I have an eternal home with Jesus, He will be with me always, even to the end of the age (Matthew 28:20). Jesus gives me eternal life and I will never perish; and no one will snatch me out of His hand. God has given me to Him, and He is greater than all; and no one is able to snatch me out of the Father's hand (John 10:28-29).

If Satan is coming at you with **feelings of Defeat – It is written**... I can be strong and courageous; I will not be afraid for the Lord my God is the one who goes with me. He will not fail me or forsake me. (Deuteronomy 31:6) If God is for me, who is against me? He who did not spare His own Son, but delivered Him over for us all, how will He not also with Him freely give us all things? Who will bring a charge against God's elect?

God is the one who justifies; who is the one who condemns? Christ Jesus is He who died, yes, rather who was raised, who is at the right hand of God, who also intercedes for us. Who will separate us from the love of Christ? Will tribulation, or distress, or persecution, or famine, or nakedness, or peril, or sword? But <u>in all these things I overwhelmingly</u>

conquer through Him who loved me (Romans 8:31-37).

If Satan has **people gossiping or backstabbing against you – It is written...** No weapon formed against me will prosper; and every tongue that accuses me in judgment I will condemn. This is the heritage of the servants of the Lord, and my vindication is from God the Lord. In righteousness I will be established; I will be far from oppression, for I will not fear; and from terror, for it will not come near me. If anyone fiercely assails me it will not be from God. Whoever assails me will fall because of me. For God has not given me the spirit of fear (Isaiah 54:17, Isaiah 54:14-15, 2 Timothy 1:7).

If Satan is **attacking your comfort and peace – It is written...** Jesus gives me His peace. So, I will not let my heart be troubled, nor let it be fearful. (John 14:27). Jesus has given me the comforter through His ever-present Holy Spirit. (John 14:6) Just as a father has compassion on his children, So the Lord has compassion on those who fear Him (Psalm 103:13).

The lovingkindness of the Lord is from everlasting to everlasting on those who fear Him, and His righteousness to children's children (Psalm 103:17).

If Satan is **attacking your joy – It is written ...** These things I have spoken to you so that My joy may be in you, and that your joy may be made full (John 15:11).

How is the enemy attacking you? Would you be willing to take time to find verses to address whatever you are facing?

Speak God's Word, His Truth, tell the enemy what is written in God's word and the enemy will flee. For **it is written**... the word of God is living and active and sharper than any two-edged sword (Hebrews 4:12). And if you will continue in God's Word, then you are truly a disciple of Christ; and you will know the truth, and **the truth will make you free** (John 8:31-23).

Cross Off

I am so very grateful for the sacrifice Jesus made by going to the cross. He took our sins and through His mercy, nailed them to the cross. Because of Jesus, we have eternal life.

How grateful I am that Jesus is NOT still on the cross. He rose again. He conquered death. His grace and mercy went to the cross, beyond the cross, to the grave, beyond the grave, rose again to give new life, new mercies, and new beginnings.

Jesus is off the cross and rose from the grave to allow us to rise anew in Him. "Therefore, if anyone is in Christ, he is a new creature; the old things passed away; behold, new things have come." ~ 2 Corinthians 5:17 (NASB)

The cross is empty, and the tomb is empty. With Jesus as our Savior, we can cross off sin's grip through Christ's grace and mercy. Jesus is the way, the truth, and the life, and He sets us free!

"For God so loved the world, that He gave His only Son, so that everyone who believes in Him will not perish but have eternal life. For God did not send the Son into the world to judge the world, but so that the world might be saved through Him." ~ John 3:16-17 (NASB)

"...God clearly shows and proves His own love for us, by the fact that while we were still sinners, Christ died for us." ~ Romans 5:8 (AMP)

Jesus "used his servant body to carry our sins to the Cross so we could be rid of sin, free to live the right way. When you were stuck in your old sin-dead life, you were incapable of responding to God. God brought you alive—right along with Christ! Think of it! All sins forgiven, the slate wiped clean, that old arrest warrant canceled and nailed to Christ's cross. And you will know the truth and the truth will set you free." ~ 1 Peter 2:24 (MSG), Colossians 2:13-14 (MSG), John 8:32 (NASB)

PAT Away Problems

We all have them – problems – small, big, and often humongous. The problems sometimes come in a line, other times in a flood. With each difficulty, we have a choice. We can whine, complain, and worry, or we can take them to the King of kings and Lord of lords.

God's word tells us to enter His courts with praise and thanksgiving. (Psalm 100:4)

Praise and thanksgiving bring us into God's presence.

"In unison when the trumpeters and the singers were to make themselves heard with one voice to praise and to glorify the Lord, and when they lifted up their voice accompanied by trumpets and cymbals and instruments of music, and when they praised the Lord saying, He indeed is good for His lovingkindness is everlasting, then the house, the house of the Lord, was filled with a cloud, so that the priests could not stand to minister because of the cloud, for the glory of the Lord filled the house of God." ~ 2 Chronicles 5:13-14 NASB

Praise and thanksgiving breaks through barriers – barriers erected by the enemy, by ourselves, by others, by our circumstances and situations. Praise and thanksgiving releases God's power!

"When they began singing and praising, the Lord set ambushes against the sons of Ammon, Moab and Mount Seir, who had come against Judah; so, they were routed." ~ 2 Chronicles 20:22 (NASB)

Praise and thanksgiving points us back to our inexhaustible power-source, all-powerful God.

Praise and thanksgiving refocuses the focus, giving new eyes, granting fresh soul-air. Praise and thanksgiving provides restoration and renewal.

P – Praise
A – And
T – Thanksgiving

So today, this very minute, PAT away your problems!

Searching for wonder

Have you ever watched a small child? The smallest object can be a source of squealing delight. A flower, a ladybug, and even a weed can capture their attention to examine, prod, and touch.

I wonder, have we lost that same wonder?

Have we stopped looking, searching, and noticing?

God has placed treasures in our every single moment, but we won't find if we don't look.

A treasure hunt isn't just a quick glance; it's an all-out pursuit, a digging, exploring, searching quest to find the amazing God-given blessings.

With the wide-eyed wonder of a small child ask to see the smallest details, seek to find the beauty, knock until the door of your heart is tender and open to notice all the blessings of God.

Search for wonder and you will see the wonders of God.

"Ask, and it will be given to you; seek, and you will find; knock, and it will be opened to you. For everyone who asks receives, and he who seeks finds, and to him who knocks it will be opened." ~Matthew 7:7-8 (NASB)

"The kingdom of heaven is like a treasure hidden in the field, which a man found and hid again; and from joy over it he goes and sells all that he has and buys that field." ~ Matthew 13:44 (NASB)

"Good friend, take to heart what I'm telling you; collect my counsels and guard them with your life.

Tune your ears to the world of Wisdom; set your heart on a life of Understanding. That's right—if you make insight your priority, and won't take no for an answer, searching for it like a prospector panning for gold, like an adventurer on a treasure hunt, believe me, before you know it Fear-of-God will be yours; you'll have come upon the Knowledge of God." ~ Proverbs 2:1-5 (MSG)

Always connected

Before leaving town for a speaking event, I drove to pick up a friend. Unfortunately, when I arrived at her house I accidentally dropped and broke my cell phone.

The break was fatal, and all phone numbers, contact information, messages, and photos stored on the device were lost. I don't know if I'll ever find some of my friend's numbers again.

I am so grateful God's number never changes, He is always available, and the only problem with a connection is when I allow sin to get in the way.

Thank You Heavenly Father that Your word promises, before we call You will answer; while we are still speaking You will hear. For there is no distinction between Jew and Greek; for the same Lord is Lord of all, abounding in riches for all who call on Him (Isaiah 65:24, Romans 10:12).

Keep Going!

Problems will come, difficulties will arise. Life can be a maze of frustrations. Persistence is key for each obstacle gives opportunity for growth and maturity. Remember whatever God has called you to do, He will be with you to supply all your needs to equip you for your journey.

Keep going!

Run the race. "Do you not know that those who run in a race all run, but only one receives the prize? Run in such a way that you may win." ~ 1 Corinthians 9:24 (NASB)

Remember God will equip you. "May the God of peace, who through the blood of the eternal covenant brought back from the dead our Lord Jesus, that great Shepherd of the sheep, equip you with everything good for doing his will, and may he work in us what is pleasing to him, through Jesus Christ, to whom be glory forever and ever. Amen. ~ Hebrews 13:20-21 (NIV)

God will supply all your needs. "And my God will supply all your needs according to His riches in glory in Christ Jesus." ~ Philippians 4:19 (NASB)

Keep your hand on the plow. "Jesus replied, 'No one who puts his hand to the plow and looks back is fit for service in the kingdom of God.' ~ Luke 9:62 (NIV)

Be diligent. "Be diligent in these matters; give yourself wholly to them, so that everyone may see your progress. Be diligent to present yourself approved to God as a workman who does not need to be ashamed, accurately handling the word of truth." ~1 Timothy 4:15 (NIV), 2 Timothy 2:15 (NASB)

Give your desires to God. "I delight to do Your will, O my God; Your Law is within my heart." ~ Psalm 40:8 (NASB)

Whatever you do, do for God's glory. "Not to us, O Lord, not to us, but to Your name give glory because of Your lovingkindness, because of Your truth." ~ Psalm 115:1 (NASB)

Make your life a freewill offering to God. "With a freewill offering I will sacrifice to you; I will give thanks to your name, O Lord, for it is good." ~ Psalm 54:6 (ESV)

Delight in God. "Delight yourself in the Lord; and He will give you the desires of your heart." ~ Psalm 37:4 (NASB)

Abound in every good work. "Grow in the grace and knowledge of our Lord and Savior Jesus Christ. To Him be the glory, both now and to the day of eternity. Amen." ~ 2 Peter 3:18 (NASB)

Fight the good fight. "Fight the good fight of faith; take hold of the eternal life to which you were called, and you made the good confession in the presence of many witnesses." ~ 1 Timothy 6:12 (NASB)

Keep zealous in working for the Lord. "Never be lacking in zeal, but keep your spiritual fervor, serving the Lord. Be joyful in hope, patient in affliction, faithful in prayer." ~ Romans 12:11-12 (NIV)

God is faithful to complete what He starts. Be "confident of this, that he who began a good work in you will carry it on to completion until the day of Christ Jesus." ~ Philippians 1:6 (NIV)

Keep going, don't give up, don't slack off, and don't let the enemy deter your walk in the Lord.

Nothing is impossible for God and there is no power, person, or situation bigger than God. Keep your focus on Christ and remember His promises, and remember He is always with you for now and through eternity. **Keep going!**

"Be brave. Be strong. Don't give up." ~ Psalm 31:23a (MSG)

Stuck in discouragement?

Several days had passed after Jesus' crucifixion and two downhearted, discouraged, and hopeless men traveled the road to Emmaus (see Luke 24:13-33). According to scholars, Emmaus was a place of "warm water used for healing."

On their way, a "stranger" approached and explained the scriptures to them on why Jesus would have to die. When they reached their destination, it seemed as though their new friend would continue on his journey, yet when they asked him in, he graciously accepted. Then when he broke bread, the men's eyes were "opened" and they recognized Jesus. The men hurried back to Jerusalem, commenting that their hearts had burned within them when Jesus had talked with them.

These men were hopeless, stuck in discouragement, and in need of some warm-water healing. However, they received so much more when they met The Healer, the Living Water who restored and reignited their hearts. They didn't just need warmth; they needed the fire of Christ. Through Him they received soul-deep, soul-repairing, hope-restoring healing.

Y'all I realized something today. These men were on the way when Jesus came to them, and they didn't even reach their destination before the fire of healing took place. Jesus stayed and came inside when invited.

I think so often we think God can't heal us of the trauma in our lives until we get to heaven.

Jesus said He came to heal the brokenhearted, to proclaim liberty to the captives, recovery of sight to the blind, and freedom for those who are oppressed.

Satan is busy breaking hearts, blinding people, and making them believe they will always be captive and won't have any opportunity for freedom on this earth. The enemy is a liar! Don't believe him!

Jesus is The Light, the Healer, The Way, He is freedom. He is The Life that brings life no matter what the enemy has done to us. God turns all things into good for those who love the Lord (Romans 8:28).

Ask Jesus into your heart. When Jesus lives in your heart, your heart has unlimited power through the power of God. Nothing is impossible for Him, and He has limitless restoration, healing, and recovery.

Are you stuck in discouragement? Need healing from your past? Don't just look for lukewarm-water healing, look to The One who is Living Water. Today, this day, dive into Jesus' unlimited, heart-burning, heart-restoring healing.

"The Spirit of the Lord is upon Me, because He has anointed Me to preach the gospel to the poor; He has sent Me to heal the brokenhearted, to proclaim liberty to the captives and recovery of sight to the blind, to set at liberty those who are oppressed; to proclaim the acceptable year of the Lord." ~ Luke 4:18-19 (NKJV)

Smile Signal

Have you ever smiled even when you really didn't feel like smiling? Did you notice you actually felt better? Have you ever been mad at something and a friend of yours says something that makes you smile or laugh? Even though you wanted to stay mad, the anger dissipates.

There's something about a smile.

Maybe a smile signals to your brain something is positive, then your brain signals to your body to lighten up, which signals to your brain that everything is going to be okay, which signals to your body, there is hope. Which signals to others that hope is found in Christ not your situation or how you feel, which causes others to smile and have hope, which signals to their brain, which signals to their mouth, which signals to their bodies, which signals back to you and others.

I know it's not always easy to smile, but please remember if Jesus lives in your heart; your heart has the joy of Jesus. And if Jesus lives in you, you definitely have a reason to smile – your sins have been forgiven and you have a guaranteed amazing happy ending!

Would you be willing to send a smile signal? You and others are waiting for that smile!

"Rejoice in the Lord always [delight, take pleasure in Him]; again, I will say, rejoice!" ~Philippians 4:4 (AMP)

Fire!

The world is on fire, and many are just standing by, not sure what to do, feeling so very helpless. The enemy is adding fuel to the fire and then intimidating anyone who comes near to try and extinguish the roaring blaze.

It's easy to feel overwhelmed by the evil in the world and downright scary to step forward to speak truth when God's truth is met with open hostility. Some days I feel like I'm holding a water pistol against a raging inferno. Then I remember, I don't hold any ordinary water or an ordinary water pistol. Jesus is The Living Water with infinite power. As His child, I can boldly speak His truth, His love, mercy, and grace to a world burning in sin and lies.

If we link hands in prayer and in speaking God's truth, we will form a bucket brigade to extinguish Satan's lies.

Not any one person has to carry the full load. Jesus is the infinite loving, living water for a world on fire.

Encourage one another, and please join me in praying and speaking God's loving truth to a world so needing God's loving truth.

"And have mercy on some, who are doubting; save others, **snatching them out of the fire**; and on some have mercy with fear, hating even the garment polluted by the flesh." ~ Jude 22-23 (NASB)

"These things I have spoken to you, so that in Me you may have peace. In the world you have tribulation but **take courage; I have overcome the world.**" ~ John 16:33 (NASB)

"Now concerning how and when all this will happen, dear brothers and sisters, we don't really need to write you. For you know quite well that the day of the Lord's return will come unexpectedly, like a thief in the night. When people are saying, 'Everything is peaceful and secure,' then disaster will fall on them as suddenly as a pregnant woman's labor pains begin. And there will be no escape. But you aren't in the dark about these things, dear brothers and sisters, and you won't be surprised when the day of the Lord comes like a thief. For you are all children of the light and of the day; we don't belong to darkness and night.

"So, **be on your guard**, not asleep like the others. Stay alert and be clearheaded. Night is the time when people sleep, and drinkers get drunk. But **let us who live in the light be clearheaded, protected by the armor of faith and love, and wearing as our helmet the confidence of our salvation.**

"For God chose to save us through our Lord Jesus Christ, not to pour out his anger on us. Christ died for us so that, whether we are dead or alive when he returns, we can live with him forever. So, **encourage each other and build each other up**, just as you are already doing." ~ 1 Thessalonians 5:1-11 (NLT)

Thinking of you

Your Heavenly Father is thinking of you...

I'm thinking of you and want you to know. I am with you. I'll watch over you wherever you go. My love for you is unfailing.

I won't ever leave or forsake you. I, your God, have a firm grip on you and I'm not letting go. I'm telling you 'Don't panic. I'm right here to help you.'

I delight in you. I will calm all your fears. I rejoice over you with joyful songs.

I love you so much I sent my Son, Jesus Christ, to pay the price for your sin.

Don't be afraid, I've redeemed you. I've called your name. You're mine.

When you're in over your head, I'll be there with you. When you're in rough waters, you will not go down. When you're between a rock and a hard place, it won't be a dead end—Because I am God, your personal God, The Holy of Israel, your Savior. I paid a huge price for you.

Jesus will return to bring you home where a place has been prepared for you.

I will wipe the tears from your eyes. There won't be any more death, mourning, or pain.

You'll drink freely of the living water, and you will be my sons and daughters, and I will be your God.

Please don't ever forget how much I love you!

Genesis 28:15 (NIV), Psalm 147:11 (NIV), Joshua 1:5 (NIV), Isaiah 41:13-14 (MSG) Zephaniah 3:17 (NLT), John 3:16 (NIV), Isaiah 43:2-4 (MSG), John 14:3 (NIV), Revelation 7:17 (NIV), Revelation 21:4 (NIV)

Splash joy!

Ever had a moment where your spirit joyfully jumps? Perhaps you see or experience something that splashes joy in your soul?

I wonder how often I squelch those blessings by staying too busy or thinking I'm far too adult to play and enjoy the moment.

What if we got up and danced a little jig?

What if we took time to look to heaven and thank God?

What if we praised Him?

What if we enjoyed the joy?

I'm passing on the joy splash! Splash with me and pass the splash of joy!

"May the Master pour on the love so it fills your lives and splashes over on everyone around you, just as it does from us to you." ~ 1 Thessalonians 3:12 MSG

Overwhelmed

Feeling overwhelmed? I have good news, no matter how overwhelmed you may feel, "overwhelming victory is ours through Christ, who loved us" (Romans 8:37 NLT).

Did you know you are a conqueror? Even better, "We are more than conquerors through him who loved us" (Romans 8:37 ESV)

You can trust God. "...I know the one in whom I trust, and I am sure that he is able to guard what I have entrusted to him until the day of his return" (2 Timothy 1:12 NLT).

Be convinced, "I am convinced that He is able ..." (2 Timothy 1:12).

Be confident. "Being confident of this, that he who began a good work in you will carry it on to completion until the day of Christ Jesus" (Philippians 1:6 NIV).

Be persuaded. "Yet he did not waver through unbelief regarding the promise of God but was strengthened in his faith and gave glory to God, being fully persuaded that God had power to do what he had promised" (Romans 4:20-21 NIV).

Live in triumph. "But thank God! He has made us his captives and continues to lead us along in Christ's triumphal procession. Now he uses us to spread the knowledge of Christ everywhere, like a sweet perfume" (2 Corinthians 2:14 NLT).

Run to win. "Don't you realize that in a race everyone runs, but only one person gets the prize? So, run to win!" (1 Corinthians 9:24 NLT).

Are you convinced you are always safe in God's Hands? "And I am convinced that nothing can ever separate us from God's love. Neither death nor life, neither angels nor demons, neither our fears for today nor our worries about tomorrow—not even the powers of hell can separate us from God's love" (Romans 8:37-38 NLT).

Heavenly Father, thank You for Your victory. I want to live as a victorious conqueror, fully trusting, convinced, confident, persuaded, living in triumph, running to win the race for I am forever safe in Your hands.

Joyfully Sharing

The last few days I've been reading and meditating on Psalm 145. Verses six and seven hit me this morning... "**Men shall speak of the power of Your awesome acts, and I will tell of Your greatness. They shall eagerly utter the memory of Your abundant goodness and will shout joyfully of Your righteousness.**" ~ Psalm 145:6-7 (NASB)*

I wonder, are we speaking of God's awesome power and greatness?

Are we eagerly telling others what God has done?

Are we shouting joyfully of His righteousness?

Please let me tell you about my awesome, powerful, great God. Let me eagerly tell you what He has done in my life and how I've seen Him beautifully work in the lives of SO many others.

I'm Joyfully SHOUTING of the righteousness of my wonderful God! Will you join me in joyfully sharing about our awesome, powerful, great God?

"But as for me, I shall sing of Your strength; yes, I shall joyfully sing of Your lovingkindness in the morning, for You have been my stronghold and a refuge in the day of my distress." ~ Psalm 59:16 (NASB)

"O come, let us sing for joy to the Lord, let us shout joyfully to the rock of our salvation." ~ Psalm 95:1 (NASB)

*(Emphasis added on scripture)

Amazing

I'm filled with wonder and questions. Each breath, every blink of an eye, each beat of our hearts reveals a miracle of God.

How does our body know how to repair itself?

How does a rose know how to form and bloom?

How does a dead seed produce a harvest?

How does a caterpillar become a butterfly?

How does our planet stay suspended in space at just the right place for people to live?

Science tries to explain away divine intervention, but they can't. They might understand some of the processes; however, no one can explain how from nothing came everything.

I may not be a scientist, I may not have an advanced degree, but I do know the most important thing —God is an amazing God!

The most amazing love is God's love. The most amazing sacrifice was made by Jesus Christ for you. The most amazing gift ever is to be His. The most amazing joy is living in the joy of Jesus.

The most amazing life is to die to self to live for Him. The most amazing purpose is to live for God's purpose. The most amazing peace is found in God's presence.

Heavenly Father, You are amazing! Thank You for your amazing love!

"Come and see what the Lord has done, the amazing things he has done on the earth." ~ Psalm 46:8 (NCV)

Wanting more

Do you want more? I want more of God. I want to be more like God's precious Son, Jesus Christ.

I'm learning, the more I get out of the way, the more God can work in me. The more I die to self, the more I can be filled with God's presence. The more I relinquish control, the more freedom I am given in Christ.

The more I yield to God's will and desires, the more God can perfect that which concerns me. The more I give Him, of me, the more He can transform me into the glory and radiance of His Son.

Because **more** than we can imagine, God loves us. "How precious to me are your thoughts, O God! How vast is the sum of them! If I would count them, they are **more** than the sand...." ~ Psalm 139:17-18 (ESV)

More than our sin, God's grace saves us. "For if while we were enemies we were reconciled to God by the death of his Son, **much more**, now that we are reconciled, shall we be saved by his life. **More** than that, we also rejoice in God through our Lord Jesus Christ, through whom we have now received reconciliation. Here it is in a nutshell: Just as one person did it wrong and got us in all this trouble with sin and death, another person did it right and got us out of it. But **more** than just getting us out of trouble, he got us into life! One man said no to God and put many people in the wrong; one man said yes to God and put many in the right." ~ Romans 5:10-12 (ESV), Romans 5:18-19 (MSG).

More than our dreams, God extravagantly blesses. "God can pour on the blessings in astonishing ways so that you're ready for anything and everything, **more** than just ready to do what needs to be done. As one psalmist puts it, He throws caution to the winds, giving to the needy in reckless abandon. His right-living, right-giving ways never run out, never wear out. This most generous God who gives seed to the farmer that becomes bread for your meals is **more** than extravagant with you. He gives you something you can then give away, which grows into full-formed lives, robust in God, wealthy in every way, so that you can be generous in every way, producing with us great praise to God." ~ 2 Corinthians 9:8-11 (MSG)

"God can do anything, you know—far **more** than you could ever imagine or guess or request in your wildest dreams! He does it not by pushing us around but by working within us, his Spirit deeply and gently within us. Glory to God in the church! Glory to God in the Messiah, in Jesus! Glory down all the generations! Glory through all millennia! Oh, yes!" ~ Ephesians 3:20-21 (MSG)

*(Emphasis added)

Please pray

Our world is a pretty messy place. Weather causes havoc, evil runs amok, and every day people are dying. We pray and ask God for relief, for help for those who are suffering, for healing, or for our list of wants and needs.

Do we remember, oh do we remember, to pray for the lost? To pray that those who don't know Jesus as Savior will know Him before it's too late.

Would you join me in praying?

Pray for those who are in peril of weather, rebels, terrorists, drought, famine, and natural disasters, that they will know Jesus.

Pray for friends, neighbors, and family members who may know God but don't have a relationship with His Son

Pray for the lost. Please pray for the lost. Pray that they will know Jesus — The Way, The Truth, and The Life.

Please remember to pray. Your prayers make a difference in the lives of others and in the world. Keep praying, friends. Please take time to pray.

"Brethren, my heart's desire and my prayer to God for them is for their salvation." Romans 10:1 (NASB)

Banquet Blessings

"He has brought me to his banquet hall, and his banner over me is love." ~ Song of Songs 2:4 (NASB).

God has prepared a banquet of love. I wonder how often I miss dining. I can get so busy and rushed; I rush right by God's blessings.

God invites us to feast on His Word, drink deep of His Living Water, and break bread with the bread of life. Instead, I've found myself under the table, out the door, or eating crumbs.

I need to slow down and remember where to find true nourishment – at His feet, in His Word, and in communion with Him in prayer.

Heavenly Father, I want to enjoy Your every blessing. Help me to spend time with You. To dine at Your banquet table so I may fill up with Your love to fill others with Your love. Help me to freely accept everything You offer so that what You give may be shared to bless others. Thank You that You bless, so we can be blessed, so others will be blessed, because with You the banquet blessings are endless!

Burn it!

Whatever is in our past, whatever we are dealing with needs to be taken to God, given to Him, and then trust He will do what needs to be done. That's not always easy. Releasing a burden or an issue from our past is hard. I've had a tendency to take something to God, lay it on His altar, then run back to pick it back up. Argh!

At times I didn't believe I had done enough for God's forgiveness, or I still needed to worry about something, or maybe I didn't ask the right way, or I just couldn't let something go from my past. I needed help in believing, remembering, and trusting. I'm a visual person, so I needed a visual.

In the Old Testament, the Israelites offered sacrifices for their sins. The sacrifice gave them the visual of flames consuming the sin that stood in the way of a relationship with a righteous and holy God. The smell, the smoke rising to Heaven, and the knowledge of that release, although probably painful to watch, had to be freeing.

In the same way, if I still have something continuing to bother or trouble me, something I just can't seem to release, I'll write it down and take it to God in prayer. Then, in a safe place, I'll burn the paper as a sacrifice. Watching the paper curl and blacken, the smoke rise to heaven, gives me a visual to remember I've taken and left those sins and concerns with God.

As the paper is consumed, I know I have placed it in God's loving care and released it to Him.

Then when the burden tries to come back, or the devil tries to remind me of something, I can visually remember my time with God. The resulting freedom is wonderful.

May I make a suggestion? If there are things you have had trouble releasing -- things you have done or things others have done to you – if you would be willing, write those things down. Not to relive the pain, but to write them to God.

Take it to God, write it out, write all that has happened, everything that is bothering you, everything you can't forgive, and everything that continues to torment, and take them to God.

Read aloud, cry, wail, and tell Him exactly how you feel about what happened, how you feel about everything. As you talk to God, ask Him to help you forgive, and lay it on His altar.

Then, if you have a safe place, burn those pages. Burn them. Watch the fire consume everything written, smell and watch the smoke as it rises to Heaven. As the edges of the papers curl, the words disintegrate; you will have a visual of your freedom.

Now when the enemy taunts you with past mistakes, or the reminder of a past sin, or past burden returns, you'll be able to remember those items have been given to God where everything falls under His justice, righteousness, and grace.

Burn it and allow God's grace, mercy, healing and restoration fire through to help you walk in His freedom.

Remove

Jesus said, "With people this is impossible, but with God all things are possible." ~ Matthew 19:26 Nothing is impossible for our God. However, in the midst of difficult situations it's often hard to remember.

During my prayer time, I realized I needed to apply this truth in my own life and in my prayers for others. I need to not only pray but proclaim God's truth in each situation to remove the things that hinder my Christian walk.

Heavenly Father ...

Remove the ache of loss, for nothing is impossible for You.

Remove the fear of the past, present, or future, for nothing is impossible for You.

Remove the pain of what others have done to me though their evil actions and evil words, for nothing is impossible for You.

Remove the sting of betrayal, for nothing is impossible for You.

Remove the worries of tomorrow, for nothing is impossible for You.

Remove any negative visuals from the past and replace them with positive visuals, for nothing is impossible for You.

Remove my focus on the things of this world to focus on You, for nothing is impossible for You.

Remove that which hinders me from running the race You have planned for me, for nothing is impossible for You.

Are you having a hard time dealing with the past, your current situation, a person or persons, or another issue? Remember, nothing is impossible for God. No difficulty is too hard, no sin too dark, no pain too deep for God to remove.

"And it will be said, 'Build up, build up, prepare the way, remove every obstacle out of the way of My people.' For thus says the high and exalted One Who lives forever, whose name is Holy, 'I dwell on a high and holy place, and also with the contrite and lowly of spirit in order to revive the spirit of the lowly and to revive the heart of the contrite." ~ Isaiah 57:14-15 (NASB)

Letter to my Father

To my Heavenly Father...

Thank You for giving me life.

Thank You for loving me even when I am so unlovely.

Thank You for granting me grace when I am so unworthy.

Thank You for Your mercy when I don't deserve mercy.

Thank You that You always want to hear my voice, and no concern is too small or too big.

Thank You for allowing me to cry on Your shoulder and to laugh and play without condemnation.

Thank You for always being available, never turning me away, and always waiting with open arms.

Thank You for Your freely offered peace and joy.

Thank You for Your loving, eternal care.

Thank You for welcoming home the prodigal children.

Thank You for Your family around the world of every race and creed.

Heavenly Father, thank You that Your love is love enough for us all.

I love You, Abba Daddy.

My heart is forever Yours.

Step

Do you need guidance and direction, for your steps? God's word is a treasure-trove of truth to help us along our journey.

God longs to guide us through His word. As we read and memorize scripture, we are blessed. The wisdom in His word promises, "When you walk about, they will guide you; when you sleep, they will watch over you; and when you awake, they will talk to you. Your ears will hear a word behind you, 'this is the way, walk in it,' whenever you turn to the right or to the left. I have directed you in the way of wisdom; I have led you in upright paths. When you walk, your steps will not be impeded; and if you run, you will not stumble." ~ Proverbs 6:22, Isaiah 30:21, Proverbs 4:11-12

God's Spirit guides us and leads us into the sweet fellowship as children of God. We no longer have to fear because we have a loving Heavenly Father. "For all who are being led by the Spirit of God, these are sons of God. For you have not received a spirit of slavery leading to fear again, but you have received a spirit of adoption as sons by which we cry out, 'Abba! Father!' Do not fear, for I am with you; do not anxiously look about you, for I am your God. I will strengthen you, surely I will help you, surely I will uphold you with My righteous right hand." ~ Romans 8:14, Isaiah 41:10

God's guidance is there for every step of the way. "The steps of a man are established by the Lord, and He delights in his way. The mind of man plans his

way, but the Lord directs his steps." ~ Psalm 37:23
Proverbs 16:9

When our steps follow Jesus, we are given
eternal life and the blessings and honor of His joyful
fellowship. As we lay down our lives to follow and
obey Him, we are blessed to have Him light our way.
Jesus said, "I am the Light of the world; he who
follows Me will not walk in the darkness but will have
the Light of life.' My sheep hear My voice, and I know
them, and they follow Me; and I give eternal life to
them, and they will never perish; and no one will
snatch them out of My hand. If anyone serves Me, he
must follow Me; and where I am, there My servant
will be also; if anyone serves Me, the Father will
honor him." ~ John 8:12, John 10:27-28, John 12:26

Even when our steps don't seem to be moving,
we can be assured as we wait... "those who wait for
the Lord will gain new strength; they will mount up
with wings like eagles, they will run and not get tired,
they will walk and not become weary. The Lord is
good to those who wait for Him, to the person who
seeks Him." ~ Isaiah 40:31, Lamentations 3:25

When we are unclear about the next steps, we
can pray as the Psalmist prayed. "Lead me in Your
truth and teach me, For You are the God of my
salvation; for You I wait all the day. Teach me Your
way, O Lord, and lead me in a level path because of
my foes. For You are my rock and my fortress; for
Your name's sake You will lead me and guide me. O
Lord, lead me in Your righteousness because of my
foes; Make Your way straight before me. O send out
Your light and Your truth, let them lead me; let them

bring me to Your holy hill and to Your dwelling places. Teach me to do Your will, for You are my God; let Your good Spirit lead me on level ground." ~ Psalm 25:5, Psalm 27:11, Psalm 31:3, Psalm 5:8, Psalm 43:3, Psalm 143:10

When we aren't sure if our steps need to move, we can pray as Moses prayed, "If Your presence does not go with us, do not lead us up from here." ~ Exodus 33:15 (We prayed this quite often with all our moves).

We are given God's light to light our way. As we read His word, even the simplest of us are blessed with His knowledge. "The unfolding of Your words gives light; it gives understanding to the simple. Your word is a lamp to my feet and a light to my path. For You light my lamp; The Lord my God illumines my darkness. The Lord is my light and my salvation; whom shall, I fear? The Lord is the defense of my life; whom shall I dread? For with You is the fountain of life; in Your light we see light." ~ Psalm 119:130, Psalm 119:105, Psalm 18:28, Psalm 27:1, Psalm 36:9

Wherever your steps may lead, remember Jesus is the Light of the world, and when you follow Him you won't walk in darkness but have the Light of life. (John 8:12)

With Jesus in your life, there will always be one lit step.

All scripture NASB unless noted.

To my readers

Thank you. I am humbled and honored you chose to read this book. I appreciate you allowing me to walk with you on this part of your journey.

I look forward to one day, sitting together and talking about our wonderful God.

Until then, keep following our heavenly Father's steps.

God bless you!

I write "not for professional theologians but for plain persons whose hearts stir them up to seek after God Himself." ~ A. W. Tozer

About the Author

Lisa Buffaloe is a happily married mom, author, and speaker. When she's not writing, she enjoys working in her yard, exploring God's beautiful nature, and taking long walks with her sweet husband.

Lisa loves sharing God's unending love and that through Him we find healing, restoration, renewal, and joy.

Visit the author at https://lisabuffaloe.com.

Books by Lisa Buffaloe

(Updated July 2023)

Fiction

The Masterpiece Beneath
Nadia's Hope (Hope and Grace Series, Book 1)
Prodigal Nights (Hope and Grace Series, Book 2)
Writing Her Heart (Hope and Grace Series, Book 3)
The Discovery Chapter (Hope and Grace Series, Book 4)
Open Lens (Hope and Grace Series, Book 5)
The Fortune
Grace for the Char-Baked

Non-Fiction

Float by Faith
Heart and Soul Medication
Time with The Timeless One
The Forgotten Resting Place
Present in His Presence
We Were Meant for Paradise

One Lit Step: Devotions for your journey
The Unnamed Devotional
Flying on His Wings
Unfailing Treasures
No Wound Too Deep for The Deep Love of Christ
Living Joyfully Free Devotional, (Volume 1)
Living Joyfully Free Devotional (Volume 2)

Thank you for reading...

One Lit Step:
Devotions for your Journey

Lisa Buffaloe